HOW TO HIT THE GROUND RUNNING IN YOUR NEW JOB

Lynda Pritchard Clemens, Ph. D.
Andrea Trulson Dolph

Printed on recyclable paper

VGM Career Horizons
a division of *NTC Publishing Group*
Lincolnwood, Illinois USA

Library of Congress Cataloging-in-Publication Data

Clemens, Lynda.
How to hit the ground running in your new job / Lynda Clemens, Andrea Dolph.
p. cm.
Includes bibliographical references.
ISBN 0-8442-4391-4
1. Vocational guidance. 2. Career development. I. Dolph, Andrea. II. Title.
HF5381.C6633 1995
650.1—dc20 94-12510
CIP

Published by VGM Career Horizons, a division of NTC Publishing Group
4255 West Touhy Avenue
Lincolnwood (Chicago), Illinois 60646-1975, U.S.A.

Manufactured in the United States of America.

4 5 6 7 8 9 0 VP 9 8 7 6 5 4 3 2 1

Contents

Section II Performance Skills 23

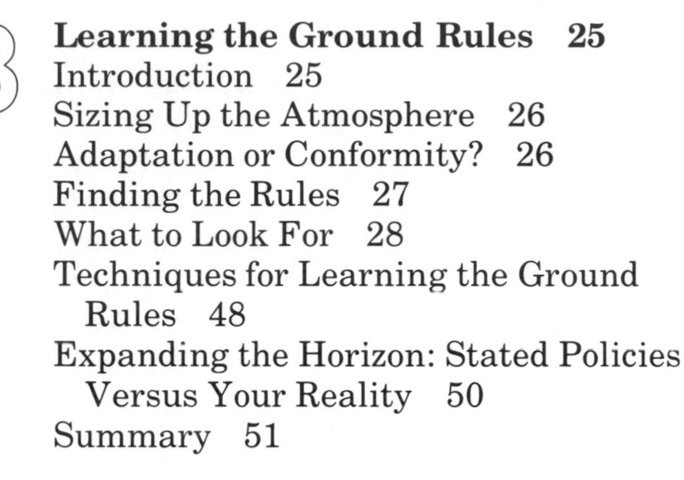

Acknowledgments

We wish to thank the many managers, supervisors, and employees who shared their experiences with us so honestly and generously. The examples used throughout this book are based on their real-life experiences, although we have combined similar stories and altered personal details to protect their privacy.

Special thanks to Claudia Groth who reviewed our manuscript and provided many helpful insights which enriched this book immensely. Finally, we acknowledge our husbands, John Dolph and Peter Clemens, who, each in his own way, inspired us to reach our goal.

Introduction: The Workplace in the 1990s

The Changing American Workplace

Will you soon be entering the workplace for the first time? Are you new to your position and finding it hard to master your job? Are you thinking of resuming your career after several years at home? Have you been an employee for some time and sense that your career has reached a plateau? Have you just changed your career path and find yourself floundering in a new professional environment? To help smooth your way in the changing American workplace, we have written this book for you.

Never before has the work environment been as challenging as employees find it today. Major upheavals are affecting American business. The resulting changes in strategies and methods of managing American companies make the employee's role more difficult than ever while—at the same time—offering new opportunities for personal growth and satisfaction on the job. There are four trends that are changing the role of employees:

1. *Downsizing.* Companies are adjusting the size of their work force to reduce the cost of doing business. This is called *downsizing* or *rightsizing.* These companies expect maximum productivity from every employee. Employees whose performance is marginal or those in businesses where profits are declining are being laid off in record numbers.

Impact on employees: Recently hired employees are expected to come up to speed faster than ever. There is also an increased chance of being laid off as certain industries adjust to changing economic circumstances. The probability of having to radically change careers is growing rapidly, as more employees are forced to shift to industries with growth opportunities. Mastering basic workplace skills is now critical to employees absorbing and adapting to these rapid changes.

2. *Delayering.* Companies are *delayering*—reducing the number of managers and the number of layers of management. This is another cost-reducing strategy since it results in fewer managers on the payroll and increased speed of decision making.

Impact on employees: On the positive side, the reduction in managers and management layers often results in the decision-making authority being pushed down to lower levels in the company. This provides employees more opportunity to directly affect the outcome of their efforts. Many enjoy this increased responsibility and challenge. A potential negative effect of delayering, particularly for a new employee, is that the *span of control* (the number of employees reporting to each manager) has increased significantly. With more employees for whom they are responsible, managers have far less time to spend on individual needs.

3. *Teaming and empowerment.* As a result of downsizing and delayering, American industry is looking for innovative ways to accomplish the same or greater work with fewer people. Giving employee teams the power to plan, conduct, and evaluate their work has become a significant trend you will have to deal with in the near future. Even if your company has not yet adopted this new concept, few industries can remain competitive without such a radical change in management philosophy.

Impact on employees: Those employees who can work in a team environment and have the skills to function with less management direction will survive and thrive in the 1990s.

4. *Increased competition.* With fewer jobs available in downsized companies, the performance criteria applied to employees are becoming increasingly stringent. More experienced employees who have been laid off are competing with new employees for the same positions. Additional competitive pressures come from international workers who may be willing to work for lower wages than American employees are.

Impact on employees: Being a satisfactory employee may no longer be enough to keep your job. Even excellent employees are in jeopardy in certain industries. These trends in the current business climate not only heighten management's need for skilled employees but also restrict availability of on-the-job training in workplace skills. Managers' expectations for employees have become more demanding because of these challenges.

Four Factors Critical to Job Performance

In order to survive in today's tough work environment, employees must demonstrate strength in all facets of their performance. The four factors that contribute to good performance in the workplace are:

- personal characteristics—attitude, ambition, integrity, and ethics
- basic mental abilities—the ability to learn, abstract, and solve problems
- skills acquired through academic training
- workplace skills not taught in schools and seldom taught directly on the job.

All four elements of the equation are necessary for successful performance.

Why We Wrote This Book

We became interested in the subject of employee performance during a recent lay-off situation in our company. Managers had to review the files of all our employees in order to rank them in terms of their past performance, their flexibility in taking on new and varied tasks, and the criticality of their skills to the business. Then all the managers met to integrate ranked lists into one complete ranking for the department. Our analysis of the discussions that took place during the creation of the integrated department ranking revealed that the fourth factor, workplace skills, was causing employees the most trouble. This proved to be true in both lay-off situations and during regular performance appraisals. We also observed that employees who had entered the work force within the past five years had the most problems with nontechnical workplace skills, seldom arriving at the workplace with the basic skills needed on the job.

Management Expectations

After the layoffs at our company, we decided to probe further into why so many employees, whether new or experienced, failed to develop workplace skills. We started by talking to a variety of managers both within and outside the company. We found that most companies did not provide any formal training in basic nontechnical skills, nor did the managers personally provide coaching in these skills to their employees. Many managers revealed that it just did not occur to them to do so. Over time, these skills had become second nature to them. It was difficult for them to understand that for many employees, workplace skills are not just a matter of common sense. Other managers explained that they simply did not have the time due to delayering initiatives at their companies. These managers needed employees who would take the initiative to observe and learn, coming to a manager only when they could not obtain specific data or guidance from other sources.

Employee Expectations

While managers require better performance on workplace skills, employees new to the work environment are not responding to the demand to learn those skills. In our discussions with a variety of employees, we discovered that few understand the challenges they face in a changing workplace. Employees were confused about where they fit into their new organizations; they were not prepared for the rules, policies, and procedures they encountered. Many employees didn't know what skills, in addition to those taught in school, they needed to learn. Others felt the pressure to perform in these areas but did not know how to go about acquiring the knowledge to do so. A surprising number did not know that they *can*—and *should*—take the initiative to ask the most basic questions they need answered. Instead, they waited to be provided orientation checklists, organization charts, and office guidelines, which were never given to them. These mistaken concepts employees had about the workplace, particularly that they would be closely supervised and individually trained, contributed to their lack of action to gain critical skills.

The Expectation Gap

It was clear from this investigation that an *expectation gap* exists between managers and new employees. Employees expected to receive more direction from their managers than they, in fact, received; managers expected to give less direction. The result of the expectation gap is that many new employees find themselves floundering in their new work environments, often making key, nontechnical errors. One young man, identified by his company as a "high potential" employee, said he sat frustrated at his desk for two weeks after receiving his first assignment because he was not sure what he had specifically been asked to accomplish. Another young woman, rather than reading the materials given to her by personnel when she joined the company, waited for direction from her manager as to how to get her relocation expenses paid. It was not until she received a note from personnel reminding her that the six-month window to submit claims for reimbursement was about to close that she panicked and asked her supervisor for guidance. The real-life examples are endless.

Furthermore, our investigation indicated that, if left to fester, poor nontechnical skills can become major liabilities. Employees who started out with extremely promising careers ended up years later as disgruntled, unsatisfactory performers because they failed to take the initiative to identify and correct their workplace skill deficiencies.

Using This Book to Bridge the Gap

In today's workplace, employees will no longer be taken care of by employers. All employees, but especially new employees, need to *take the initiative* to understand their particular business and organization, acquire the workplace skills taught in this book, and manage their own careers. This book is designed to help new employees identify and practice specific workplace skills so that they may take charge of their career destiny. You can improve performance on the job by:

- developing proficiency in workplace skills through mastering the chapters, completing the exercises, and referring to recommended additional reading;
- adapting the skills to your individual work environment;
- returning to specific chapters to reinforce your abilities as you gain more experience.

INTRODUCTION TO THE WORKPLACE

Section I

Getting a Head Start

Introduction

No matter what academic major you studied, there are additional basic proficiencies expected on any job. Excuses—such as "I've never been very good in math" or "I just hate writing down my thoughts" or "I'm afraid to speak in front of an audience"—are unacceptable in a place of business. In this chapter we explain the core set of skills you will need in the workplace, why you need them, various ways you can acquire them, and how to find risk-free opportunities to practice these skills and other skills related to work.

Eight Core Skills for the Workplace

There are eight basic skills that are core competencies for the workplace.

1. *Etiquette*

Good manners provide the grease that helps business interactions to function smoothly. Despite our casual lifestyle, which seldom calls for the use of formal etiquette rules, manners still matter. During your job interviews and on the job, people will be assessing you for your assurance or lack thereof in handling common social situations.

2. *English*

The quality of your oral and written communications mark you as a well or poorly educated person. Although ending a sentence with a preposition is no longer the sin it used to be, composing a grammatical sentence is still important to make your audience understand you and for the impression you leave with others. The use of such terms as "irregardless" (this is *not* a word) can focus your audience on your grammar rather than the content of your message. If you frequently make these kinds of errors, you lose credibility.

Skill in spelling is not just following the rules, but also understanding the meaning of words. The common misuse of *their, there* and *they're* is a good example of how poor grammar can combine with poor spelling to compound a mistake. When presented with these types of mistakes, the reader has the impression that the author is either extremely careless or uneducated.

Knowing how to properly punctuate puts the finishing touch to your written communications. The proper use of commas, quotation marks, and parentheses helps the reader to follow your thoughts and clarifies your message.

3. *Mathematics*

Adding, subtracting, multiplying, and dividing without a calculator is becoming a lost art. Understanding percentages, decimal arithmetic, and basic statistics allows you to confidently prepare your own work and analyze the work of others. If you can quickly calculate a tip at lunch, divide the check among an odd number of people, or point out a serious mistake during a meeting, you will impress your co-workers and increase their confidence in your abilities.

4. *Public speaking*

Nothing brings terror to the heart of most people like the need to give a speech. The most experienced public speakers admit that they never really conquer their nervousness before an audience. In addition, unless public speaking is a regular part of your job, this skill cannot develop and improve on the job. Nevertheless, companies call upon most employees to give an occasional speech or presentation to a group. Your skill level in this arena will be duly noted and appraised. How well you present material to a group can affect whether or not your manager selects you for particular assignments or positions.

5. *Typing*

With the arrival of personal computers, large companies are funding fewer secretaries or typing pools. In smaller companies, typing your own letters and reports is often the norm. Electronic mail systems are becoming commonplace and require that you type your messages yourself. Although you need not acquire the speed expected of those who perform typing as a major function in their job, you must know the standard keyboard and be able to produce an error-free memo.

6. *Computer literacy*

There is hardly an area of business that does not use computers in some fashion. Whether it is recording retail point-of-sale information or producing documents with a word processor, the use of computers is here to stay and will become even more important in the future. If you cannot use the basic functions of a personal computer—word processing, spreadsheets, and database—you will have a difficult adjustment to make. Without a basic understanding of how computers and computer programs function, you will have trouble learning more sophisticated programs, such as project management or scheduling packages, which your job may require. With all the other aspects of the job that a new employee must learn, having to also learn computer processing can seriously impede your performance.

7. *Teamwork*

"Teamwork" is a significant business trend in the 1990s. Businesses are reducing the number of managers. They expect employees, working as a team, to perform various functions, such as achieving productivity and quality improvements, scheduling and performing work, and solving business problems, which formerly managers performed. Your ability to function as a team member helps the organization achieve its goals. Businesses often assign routine tasks and fewer responsibilities to employees who cannot work with others for a common goal. They may not consider such employees for promotions.

8. *Leadership*

Even with an increased emphasis on teamwork, the business world values leaders. Teams can perform best when a natural—rather than management-selected—leader emerges from the team. Experienced leaders understand how to help a team arrive at common goals and objectives, solve problems, make decisions, and plan and execute tasks, as well as handle the interpersonal issues inherent in any team situation.

Use the following "Checklist: What Do You Know?" to evaluate where you are now in terms of basic business proficiencies, and what you need to do to increase your skill level.

Checklist: What Do You Know?

Skill	Do you know how to . . . ?	Yes/ No	How to learn the skill
1. Etiquette	• Bring your napkin to your lap at the proper time? • Accept and return the menu to the waitperson? • Give your order for the meal? • Use the correct knife, fork, or spoon when the table is set with more than one of each? • Select when to pick up the check and when not to? • Order wine? • Accept or reject the wine when it arrives at the table? • Introduce yourself to a stranger? • Introduce a customer to a coworker? • Introduce a man to a woman or a woman to a man? • Introduce a younger person to an older person? • Shake hands with someone of the same and someone of the opposite sex? • Open doors for others? • Exit an elevator? • Decide whether or not to stand?		Buy, read, and frequently consult a good book on etiquette.
2. English	• Use the following homonyms correctly? too/to/two their/there/they're where/wear/ware sight/site/cite • Use affect and effect in a sentence? • Make the subject and verb in a sentence agree? • Use it's and its?		Buy, read, and frequently consult several good books on grammar and spelling. Emulate your professors or other well-spoken people.

Skill	Do you know how to . . . ?	Yes/ No	How to learn the skill
	• Decide when to use the following? who, which, or that since or because good or well can or may lie or lay • Avoid the passive voice? • Identify and fix a double negative? • Use commas, semicolons, colons, parentheses, hyphens, question marks, and periods?		Read quality publications. Do not assume that printed media or what is said on television is correct and can be followed as an example. Buy a dictionary and use it! Use software that will check your spelling. Play scrabble, do crossword puzzles, and play other word games.
3. Mathematics	• Calculate the tip at a restaurant in your head? • Divide a $14.25 lunch bill among 3 people, without a calculator? • Check the result of a calculation to see if it is "reasonable" (determine if a major mathematical error has been made)? • Add, subtract, multiply, and divide fractions? • Calculate percentages? • Determine the number of unique combinations that could be made if 10 items were paired? • Calculate the mean, median, and mode for a set of data, and when to use which calculation?		Attend a remedial workshop or night course. Go back to those old mathematics books you saved and learn the mathematical functions you have forgotten.
4. Public speaking	• Control your voice and use it for emphasis? • Make eye contact with everyone in the audience? • Capture an audience's attention? • Answer questions from the audience? • Get your message across in the first two minutes of your presentation?		Join Toastmasters, a nationwide organization. Attend a public speaking class. Practice, practice, practice.

Skill	Do you know how to . . . ?	Yes/ No	How to learn the skill
5. Typing	• Set margins and tabs? • Identify the positions of the keys without looking at the keyboard? • Use correct keying techniques (yes, all ten fingers!) when typing? • Produce an error-free memo in 10 to 15 minutes on a standard keyboard?		Attend an introductory computer course where typing is part of the curriculum. Find a personal computer program or video tape that teaches typing. Attend a course at a technical or business school.
6. Computer literacy	• Use the function keys on a personal computer? • Set up a spreadsheet? • Use a word processing software package? • Enter and retrieve data from a database software package? • Install software on a personal computer? • Follow the documentation for the software? • Troubleshoot a personal computer problem?		Attend a course at a technical or business school. Buy, rent, or borrow a personal computer.
7. Teamwork	• Participate in a group without trying to control the group's activities? • Compromise to achieve a team's goal? • Accept and implement the ideas of other team members when they don't agree with yours? • Trust team members to perform without your help or supervision? • Give team members constructive feedback without hurting their feelings? • Be satisfied with a team's success without having any personal recognition for your contribution to the result?		Participate in team sports. Participate in social and professional organizations.

Skill	Do you know how to . . . ?	Yes/ No	How to learn the skill
8. Leadership	• Inspire others to work toward a common goal? • Identify the strengths and weaknesses of others and assign tasks appropriately? • Coach and mentor others to overcome their weaknesses? • Identify problems and communicate them? • Listen to the recommendations of others when trying to solve a problem? • Reject someone's ideas while maintaining the person's support?		Hold office in a social or professional organization.

Finding Risk-Free Opportunities to Practice Core Skills

Whether or not you are still a student, there are many risk-free opportunities to learn and practice these basic proficiencies, as well as practice all the other job-related skills we teach in this book. Participating in sports, service or volunteer organizations, student or local government, or other extracurricular activities, offers you the chance to exercise your emerging skills. Whether you are a leader in these activities or an individual contributor, you can test your wings to determine your strengths and weaknesses, your likes and dislikes, and to develop new skills and abilities with no adverse effect on your permanent job performance.

If You Are Still a Student

Take advantage of summer jobs, work-study programs, and internships to learn about a variety of work environments before selecting a permanent position. Temporary work experiences give you an opportunity to practice skills related to work and to evaluate your personal work style preferences. To your surprise, you may find you prefer working outdoors or with young people, or with detailed data. Holding a variety of temporary positions allows you to explore work options you may never have considered. Determining early on the kinds of work you enjoy and the kinds that you do not will help you select a permanent position better suited to your interests and abilities. Because any mistakes you make do not become part of your permanent job record, you can experiment with a variety of approaches to the workplace. You can practice deciphering the organizational structure, accepting an assignment, receiving feedback, and planning and executing tasks, knowing that you will be back in school soon. Even if you are interested in a permanent position with the company, the mistakes you make will probably be attributed to your lack of experience and overlooked.

Other benefits to temporary jobs include the opportunity to visit new locations, acquaint yourself with a strange city, meet new people, and independently manage your money. Depending on your background, you may be more or less self-reliant and independent. Temporary positions allow you to develop these traits while maintaining the safety net of school and family.

A Semester Abroad and Other Travel

Participating in a semester as a foreign exchange student can broaden your horizons and further test your resiliency. You will learn to appreciate and experience other cultures and lifestyles; perhaps learn or practice a foreign language; or see firsthand the wonders of art, history, and geography you have only read about. Take advantage of this kind of program if the opportunity affords itself. Although some of these experiences may require additional financial burdens beyond your school loans, you can benefit in ways that cannot be easily quantified. Picture yourself at a job interview discussing the emerging Russian free-enterprise system, the pros and cons of social medicine as practiced in Sweden, or the beauty of the Parthenon. The average job candidate cannot compete with this kind of experience.

Before accepting a permanent work position, consider volunteering in the Peace Corps, VISTA (Volunteers in Service to America), or other government-sponsored programs. Serving in the armed forces is yet another avenue for pre-career experiences that can benefit your personal growth and thus your permanent employment success.

Summary

Acquiring the eight core skills described in this chapter ensures that you have a firm foundation for the workplace. In the rapidly changing world of work, these competencies will help you adapt to changes in technology, the marketplace, and business cycles.

Whatever means you choose to acquire and practice these basic skills, taking advantage of risk-free experiences demonstrates your flexibility, openness, and independent spirit to potential employers. The experiences you gather by opening your horizons on many fronts will prove invaluable in the future. The only bad experience you can have in these risk-free arenas is the one you fail to learn from.

Quick Tips for a Good First Impression

Introduction

In a layoff situation, it is astonishing to see the importance often placed on simple mistakes made early in a person's career. Layoff committee members will frequently refer to their perceptions of people from years earlier during employee evaluation sessions. Employees who show inexperience in business settings can be added to the list of layoff candidates because they appear awkward when meeting or conversing with new people, fail to show expected business etiquette, or dress inappropriately for the office. Although a layoff committee will ultimately apply more objective criteria, this example of the lingering effects of first impressions shows how important this topic is to new employees.

You do not have to be in a layoff situation to be affected by a poor first impression. Many companies are using new approaches to appraising employee performance. They now solicit information from other managers, peers, and customers who interact with employees. This new approach makes every encounter, no matter how brief or casual, an opportunity to make a positive or negative impression that can have lasting consequences.

Tips on Appearance

There are a number of ways to ensure that your personal appearance, as well as that of your possessions and work area, meets the expectations of your business associates.

Invest in your teeth. A winning smile makes a great first impression. Follow your dentist's advice—brush, floss, and have your teeth cleaned regularly.

Bathe regularly. Body odor is a turnoff. Make personal hygiene a regular part of your routine, including washing your hair and having frequent haircuts.

Maintain your nails. Keep your nails clean and groomed. Excessive nail length or bold nail polish distracts others from their focus on you as a worker.

Groom in private. Do not freshen your makeup, clean your nails, or comb your hair in public. Go to the washroom.

Dress like the gang. Modify your dress to fit in to the business environment where you work. Sloppy, overly dressy, or revealing clothing is never appropriate in the office.

Match jewelry to attire. Jewelry should enhance, not distract from, the overall style of your office attire. This applies to both men and women.

Moderate your accent. North, south, east, west, foreign, or ethnic, we all have an accent. The closer your speech comes to a more neutral example of standard pronunciation, the more clearly you can communicate with people.

Keep your desk neat. "A neat desk is the sign of a sick mind," says the comical wall plaque. Actually, either extreme—a desk devoid of paper or one with mounds of papers and no work space—can make a bad impression. If your desk is empty, it appears that you do nothing or have nothing to do. If your desktop isn't even visible, you appear disorganized and overwhelmed. File papers regularly and keep current work in folders where it's organized and readily available.

Decorate tastefully. Keep sexist, racist, or other offensive material out of your office space. Do not display posters or other material that may appear immature or offensive in an office environment.

Lower the radio. If you are allowed to have a radio in your office space, be considerate of others. Keep the volume low and avoid music with heavy bass—the vibrations can drive your coworkers to distraction.

Clean your car. At any time, someone may ask you for a ride to a meeting or lunch. Keep your car clean inside and out. Remove offensive bumper stickers.

Keep your illness to yourself. Coming to work when you are seriously ill suggests you are insensitive to the well-being of others. If you must come to work, remember that germs are spread in the air and by direct contact.

Tips on Social Situations

You will engage in social, as well as business, encounters with managers and coworkers. Following these tips will leave others with the impression that you are socially adept and a caring, considerate person.

May I introduce. . . . Learn to introduce yourself and others with regard to their age, sex, and position in relation to yours.

Remembering names. When introduced to someone, use his or her name several times in the subsequent conversation. This will help you remember the name in the future, as well as make the person feel you have taken a personal interest.

Use first names correctly. This is *tricky*! If you are told "We are all on a first-name basis around here," the problem of when to use first names may seem solved. However, if a person's title or responsibilities were included in the introduction (for example, "This is Susan Smith, head of manufacturing), it is probably wise to reply "Nice to meet you, Ms. Smith." Let the person invite you to be on a first-name basis; don't assume you should be. On the other hand, when there are context cues which indicate you are meeting a peer (for example, "This is John Brown. John will be helping you get settled for the first couple of weeks."), use the more friendly first name.

Shake hands firmly. Learn to shake hands with both the same and opposite sex with a firm, dry handshake.

Share lunch times. Lunch with a variety of people. This is an opportunity to meet many different coworkers and get to know them better.

Use good table manners. When lunching with others, use good table manners. If you are unsure which fork to use or when to place your napkin in your lap, refer back to Chapter 1 for ways to learn these social standards.

Do you eat at your desk? Whether or not you may eat lunch at your desk will depend on the norms of the office. If others do eat at their desks, but your job requires you to sit where visitors or customers can see you, eat your lunch elsewhere.

When lunching at your desk, be sensitive to any lingering food odors that your choice of food may create. Avoid onions and other foods with strong odors. Dispose of the wrappings where they will not bother others for the rest of the afternoon.

Do you read at your desk? Reading at your desk during the lunch hour is another behavior that depends on office norms. Reading the newspaper when no one else does, either before work or during lunch, gives the appearance that you are just putting in time, not working.

Make the coffee. Take your turn making the coffee. Never take the last cup and put the pot back empty. This is a small act of teamwork and consideration that others will notice.

Resist gossiping. The office grapevine often includes more than business rumors. Do not engage in personal gossip about your coworkers or managers.

Never borrow money. Do not discuss or conduct personal finances in the office. Borrow money only from family or friends not associated with your work.

Do you bet at work? Office pools come in many varieties. Betting on sports pools is illegal in many states and many offices forbid it.

Do you give or not? Gift collections for births, deaths, and weddings are common events in the office. Give if you can afford it; politely decline if you cannot, but be consistent in your giving habits so you appear fair and evenhanded.

Don't smoke. Smoking is less accepted than ever. If you don't smoke, don't start. If you do, quit now! If you must smoke, be considerate of others and take it outside.

Do you chew gum? Many people, especially smokers, chew gum in the office. Limit your chewing habit to your office area. Avoid large wads of gum and the accompanying loud chewing noises.

Curb your drinking. Drinking at lunch can impair your performance. Mints will not disguise your altered behavior. Drinking can cost you your reputation or worse—your job. Drinking too much during office parties or other social events can be dangerous in many ways. Not only do you jeopardize your reputation, your loss of inhibition may find you saying and doing things that you cannot undo.

Avoid controversy. Politics and religion are dangerous subjects in the office. Don't offend others by constantly arguing your personal viewpoints. There are two sides to every story and your coworkers are entitled to their opinions, just as you are. The office is not the place to try to convert or reform people.

Tips on Business Etiquette

These tips on business etiquette provide the basic guidelines for business interactions that will make you appear confident and savvy.

Focus on business. Minimize personal business at the office.

Keep appointments. Being late sends a message that you do not respect the other person's time. Buy a watch with an alarm if you are perpetually late for meetings and appointments. Learn to be aware of time.

Know how to cancel appointments. Sometimes you must cancel or reschedule an appointment. Try to give advance warning of such a situation. Be sure to ask when it would be convenient to reschedule the meeting.

Carry an appointment book. Keep your appointment book with you at all times. This allows you to make appointments immediately, without having to return to your desk.

Keep busy. Carry a folder of work and a pad of paper with you. If you are kept waiting for an appointment or meeting to start, you will be able to make good use of the time.

Don't linger. When you stop by to see someone, do not hang in the doorway if they are on the phone or with someone else. Unless they signal you to stay, return at a more convenient time.

Don't overstay your welcome. Whether on a scheduled appointment or a drop-in visit, be sensitive to how much time you are taking. Be alert for signals from others, such as shuffling papers or looking at the time, which indicate it is time for you to wrap up your business or conversation and leave.

Never snoop. It is so tempting when dropping something off in an empty office or picking up reports from a printer to glance over papers left lying about. If someone catches you snooping, however, you will have lost the trust of at least one person and risk others being told of your dishonesty.

Respect everyone. Treat everyone you meet with the same respect you would show to the president of the company. Secretaries, in particular, are sensitive to whether or not you respect their responsibilities and abilities. Secretaries have more power to make or break you than you may currently appreciate.

Stifle stereotypes. Do not make assumptions concerning who strangers might be. All managers are not older white males; all secretaries are not young females. These stereotypes do not belong in the office environment.

Embrace diversity. A counterpart to stifling stereotyping is embracing diversity. Never tell a joke when the supposed humor is at the expense of others. Whether the joke or comment involves sexual, racial, or ethnic stereotypes or pokes fun at someone's age, height, weight, hair loss, religion, physical limitation, or personal quirk, you will have belittled yourself rather than others.

Appreciate others. Use "Please" and "Thank you" in your business interchanges. This will create goodwill among those with whom you work.

Answer courteously. Consistently answer your phone in a professional manner. Use your name and place of business in your greeting.

Show your interest. Attend general meetings, educational sessions, and office parties held outside office hours. Attendance may appear optional but showing interest in these activities helps to establish your credibility as a serious worker.

Ease up on your ego. No matter how much you have previously accomplished in school, you are just another new employee to your coworkers. Coworkers will resent any displays of ego. This can lead to disruptive business relationships.

Chill your emotions. Excessive displays of emotion, whether positive or negative, are inappropriate in the workplace. Learn to control your emotions and channel them into professionally appropriate comments and behaviors. Never take it out on coworkers if you are having a bad day.

Avoid foul language. Cursing is offensive to many people. Do not use vulgar or otherwise offensive language in the office.

Make eye contact. Looking people in the eye when speaking to them conveys your honest, open character. Shy people must learn to use this technique, no matter how difficult. Break eye contact periodically. Staring implies hostility or confrontation.

Learn to listen. Anxiety over composing the best possible response can keep people from truly listening to others. Be an *active* listener by paraphrasing what was said to you, making appropriate eye contact, and using a moderate amount of nonverbal signals, such as head nodding and leaning toward the speaker.

Monitor conversations. Never hold a conversation which should be kept private in a public area, such as the wash room, elevator, or lounge. You never know who can overhear your remarks. Private conversations include those critical of others in any way, those critical of management or business practices, and those addressing sensitive areas, such as the salary, job performance, or promotion of others.

Never ask about someone's salary. The salary of your coworkers is no concern of yours. Despite your curiosity and desire to compare what you are earning with the salary of others, this information is strictly off-limits in a business environment. Do not tell others what you are making. Sharing salary information is a major breach of business etiquette.

Summary

The old adage says that you never get a second chance to make a good first impression. How others perceive you, especially when they first meet and interact with you, can influence all subsequent contacts between you. We have provided some basic tips for you to follow to make a positive first impression. If you have further concerns in this area, solicit constructive feedback from a trusted friend or family member. Before you do, however, be sure you are open to receiving both positive feedback and feedback about areas in which you need to improve. Chapter 6, "Performance Feedback and Compensation," describes how to prepare to learn from such an open and frank discussion.

PERFORMANCE SKILLS

Section II

Learning the Ground Rules

Introduction

You've been on the job for several days. You and your supervisor have discussed your job responsibilities. You've met some coworkers, have a desk, and may have a "buddy" to help you learn the ropes. Now what do you do? New employees often focus all their attention on learning how to perform immediate tasks. It is true that you won't succeed if you don't perform your assigned tasks well. However, your work occurs within a context. Each work environment has a unique *culture,* or way of life. This culture reflects business goals and values, expects performance to meet a set of standards, operates within an organizational structure, and even has its own language, full of jargon and acronyms.

Sizing Up the Atmosphere

Like an anthropologist set down on an isolated island, you must learn the rules of your new culture to fit in and successfully perform your tasks. Some of the rules will be obvious—on Fridays, everyone in the office dresses casually. Others will not. Sometimes written goal statements, policies, and procedures will conflict with what you observe or experience. In this chapter, the various aspects of the culture that you must actively seek to understand will be explained. Techniques are included to aid in your study of your new situation, and suggestions are made to keep you from making serious mistakes while learning about your new environment.

Adaptation or Conformity?

In recommending that you adapt to the office culture, you are not being told to suppress everything unique about your background, personality, preferences, or outlook. Businesses are becoming more aware of the natural diversity in the workforce. Minorities are being actively recruited for their different strengths and perspectives. We are not addressing minority issues *per se* but rather adaptations to established norms.

To illustrate, take the case of a rather superficial behavior—what you wear to the office. There are businesses, such as banking, that expect you to follow certain conservative dress and grooming codes. They feel that more conservative-appearing individuals give the impression that they are more responsible. Right or wrong, the issue for banks is establishing public trust in handling financial affairs. In this business culture, males with ponytails and earrings or females with spike haircuts and mini skirts do not project the desired conservative image. On the other hand, in a research and development organization, a banker's charcoal gray suit and white shirt or blouse might appear totally out of place. This style of dress implies a more rigid, conventional approach than that desired in a research organization. Can you deviate from your organization's norms? Certainly! However, you should be aware of the potential consequences of your actions.

Advantages of Adapting

Learning your business' culture will do more than help you pick out your clothes in the morning. It will help you to determine how to behave, who to associate with, how to get your job done effectively, where to go for help, and—most importantly—whether or not you will fit into the organization. If an organization's culture is in conflict with your personal objectives, values, work habits, and career aspirations, you will not find the job satisfaction you seek.

If you modify your behavior to adapt to your organization's culture, people will quickly accept you as a member of the group. If you do not, you may find your acceptance to be more difficult but certainly not impossible. You must decide for yourself how willing you are to conform to gain quick acceptance from your supervisor and coworkers.

Finding the Rules

Whether simple or complex, formal or informal, large or small, your new organization will probably have some written materials that document the organization's goals, values, standards, policies, procedures, and structure. Some sources are:

- your supervisor;
- fellow employees, especially secretaries, the technical publications organization, or your "buddy," if you were assigned one;
- the personnel department, also called *human resources;*
- company publications, including newsletters and magazines;
- the technical library (if your organization has one);
- external sources of business analysis, such as the *Wall Street Journal* (for larger companies) or the local business press. Public libraries often keep files on local businesses, which you may find very useful.

Finding and reading this written information will save you enormous amounts of time and energy. Some organizations even have a special publication for new employees that may include maps of the building(s), forms and procedures for obtaining needed resources (for example: a phone, computer log-on identifier, office supplies), and a list of whom to contact for standard office problems.

Many managers fail to give out these materials when introducing someone to the organization. You may have to ask if they are available. You may even have to ask for the office phone directory! No one is trying to keep this information from you. They have simply forgotten how much there is to learn about the organization because they are so familiar with it.

What to Look For

When everything about the workplace is new to you, what should you begin to focus on so you are not overwhelmed? Here are some areas to investigate, including why they will be important to you.

Identifying Company Values and Goals

By reading company publications, such as mission statements, organization charts, memos describing yearly goals and objectives, and, especially, company newsletters and magazines, you will begin to find recurring themes.

Common themes are "top quality," "customer service," "productivity," or "return on investment." These types of themes reflect the goals, values, and directions the company executives consider critical to the business. Sometimes the messages are obvious and sometimes they are very subtle.

To test your skills in abstracting themes from company publications, here are two company newsletters from the mythical TNT and PDQ companies.

First read each newsletter, *TNT News* (**Exhibit 3.1**) and *PDQ News* (**Exhibit 3.2**). Then answer the quiz questions for each (**Exhibits 3.3** and **3.4**). The answers are provided in **Exhibit 3.5**, but test your skill first!

Exhibit 3.1. ***TNT News***

TNT NEWS

June 1994

QUALITY—key to maintaining TNT's competitive edge

The need to improve quality at TNT was the theme of the annual address given by Ray Barker, CEO, at the recent management off-site meeting. Mr. Barker told the assembled managers, representing all the TNT divisions, that global competition requires an increased emphasis on zero defects. "Our market share depends on our ability to produce products that provide the highest quality at the least cost," said Mr. Barker. Mr. Barker named Senior Vice President, Caroline Stewart, to head up a task force to implement a Zero Defect Program.

Ms. Stewart received a degree in Electrical Engineering from Howard University in 1974 and joined TNT in 1976 as a Research Engineer. During her career, she has held various posts at TNT, including Micro Products Manager, Business Development Manager, and Quality Control Manager. "I believe that zero defects is an achievable goal by year end if we all work as a team to uncover the source of our quality problems," said Ms. Stewart.

Sonia Garcia named *TNT Engineer of the Year*

Sonia Garcia, Senior Engineer from the Engineering Division, was selected *TNT Engineer of the Year* for her outstanding contributions to new product development. Ms. Garcia's product designs ". . . were a significant contribution to our recent proposals on the AWUS, IGE and RSU contracts," said Joan Smith, Engineering Division Manager.

TNT benefits update

The recently negotiated contract with Local 121 resulted in a number of changes to the TNT benefits package. Employees can now select the benefits they wish to participate in using a "cafeteria" type approach. Employees will also be contributing a larger percentage of the cost of medical insurance through payroll deductions. Formerly, TNT paid the entire cost but increasing medical costs "must be shared between the employee and the company," said Sandy Jackson, Employee Relations Manager.

Ms. Jackson stated that the flexibility of the cafeteria approach allows each employee to "maximize the use of each benefit dollar because employees select the benefits which are most appropriate to their personal circumstances." For example, single employees with no family obligations may reduce the amount of life insurance provided and increase the company contribution to their savings plan instead. Employees with young children may select a special saving option for future educational expenses in lieu of larger retirement benefits. Lunchtime briefings will be held during July to provide further information.

Stu Gold announces recent award winners

Stu Gold, Quality Control Manager, recently cited the Electronic Assembly Test Team for their innovative work in reducing the time required for testing assemblies by 25% while exceeding contract tolerance re-

(continued)

Exhibit 3.1. (continued)

quirements. The team, consisting of Sue Myers, John Jones, Mary Johnson, Mike Campbell and Andy Kraus, received certificates of merit, as well as cash awards. Mr. Gold summed up the team's contribution as ". . . the kind of creative problem solving which will enhance our ability to reduce costs and win contracts."

TNT annual family picnic planned

The annual TNT picnic will be held on Saturday, July 12 at Rumpole Park from noon to dusk. Bring the family and enjoy swimming, tubing, volleyball, softball, hiking, and lots of good food. Rain date is Saturday, July 19th.

Data processing centers outscored

John Morgan, Data Processing Manager, has negotiated a contract with ATA Industries for all computer center functions starting with manufacturing in January, 1993. ATA will centralize data processing for TNT. "TNT can no longer afford to maintain support staff in multiple locations. ATA offers us quality services at a greatly reduced cost." Plans to transfer the work are under development. This change will affect 56 data processing personnel at the various locations. Management is hoping to avoid layoffs through reassignments, special early retirement packages, and voluntary attrition. Mr. Morgan plans to consolidate and outsource data processing for all of TNT by the end of 1993.

Teamwork training offered

Sandy Jackson, Employee Relations Manager, will hold *Teamwork* training courses for the Northeast Division throughout the rest of 1992. The *Teamwork* initiative, started in 1991 to enable employees to take responsibility for the entire product manufacturing process, has proven a major success in the Southwest Division. "Product cycle time has been reduced by 50% in many cases," says Ms. Jackson, "while the number of supervisors was significantly reduced. The result is greater employee satisfaction, as well as reduced costs."

Teamwork classes are held one day a week for 8 weeks. Interested employees should inform their manager and contact Ms. Jackson at ext. 5656.

Around the industry . . .

RQO, Inc. teaming with Samon Company, has been awarded the 55 million dollar contract for the Air Force electronic standardization program. TNT's design was eliminated from the competition in the first round evaluations earlier this year due to technical problems.

Tamac, Ltd. beat TNT on cost to win a contract with Saudia Arabia to upgrade and manage their nuclear power plants.

Kokyo Electronics, Inc. announced the introduction of an advanced video disc player which will compete directly with TNT's *Video-Disc* product line. Amy Sokol, Manager, Consumer Electronics, expects the Kokyo product to "capture the imagination of the public and a major market share. TNT must devote more resources to basic research in order to compete in this area."

Around the company . . .

Susan Morgan, daughter of John Morgan, Data Processing Manager, is the recipient of the 1992 TNT Merit Scholarship award.

(continued)

Exhibit 3.1. (continued)

Susan, a straight A student, is president of her class, a varsity tennis player, champion chess master and co-chair of her high school science club. She will attend the University of Pennsylvania, majoring in civil engineering in the fall. Father John says, "She's a very special person and her mother and I are very proud."

Ray Barker, CEO, will reward any employee who quits smoking for one year with an extra week's vacation. Mr. Barker told us "I strongly recommend that all employees who smoke call their local staff physician and join TNT's Quit NOW! Program. It worked for me!"

Service anniversaries:
Bob Bell—30 years
Betty Rollins—25 years
Paul Zatz—25 years
Tony Dale—20 years
Padjma Bolt—20 years
Meg Evans—10 years
Jane Hunter—10 years
Jim Fisher—10 years
Binh Khuu—10 years
Robin Murphy—5 years
Carl Palma—6 years

Births:
Meg and John Evans—a daughter, Mary
Betty and Joe Hines—a son, Jeffery
Mike and Mary King—a son, George

Deaths:
Randy Jackson—retired
Ron Stevens—retired
Linda Jones

Exhibit 3.2. ***PDQ News***

PDQ NEWS

June 1994

Marketing—key to maintaining PDQ's competitive edge

The need to improve marketing at PDQ was the theme of the annual address given by Raymond Appleberry, CEO, at the recent management off-site. Mr. Appleberry told the assembled managers, representing all the PDQ divisions, that increased competition and a shrinking market requires an increased emphasis on marketing and sales. "Our market share depends on our ability to convince our customers we provide the highest quality at the lowest cost," said Mr. Appleberry. Mr. Appleberry named Senior Vice President, J. Sean Branton, to develop and implement a new marketing strategy and sales training program.

Mr. Branton received a degree in Electrical Engineering from New York University in 1974 and an MBA from the Wharton School of the University of Pennsylvania in 1979. He joined PDQ in 1979 as a Sales Representative. During his career, he has held various posts at PDQ, including Northeast Regional Sales Manager, New Business Development Manager, and Marketing Manager. "I believe that a fresh approach will increase sales 20% by year end," said Mr. Branton.

Training courses offered

Thomas Jackson, Employee Relations Manager, has contracted MPP Consultants to conduct training courses for new managers starting in October, 1992. Topics include scheduling and budgeting, resource management, production improvement techniques, and employee motivation and appraisal techniques. New Manager classes will be held every Friday for 8 weeks. Similar classes will also be held for supervisors and project leaders starting in November. Managers can enroll their eligible employees by contacting Mr. Jackson at ext. 5656.

Data processing centers outsourced

John Morgan, Data Processing Manager, has negotiated a contract with ATA Industries for all computer center functions. ATA will take over all data processing for PDQ by the end of the year. "PDQ can no longer afford to maintain these kinds of support staffs in the face of rising overhead costs. ATA offers us comparable services at a greatly reduced cost." The computer center will be closed and 56 data processing personnel will be laid off by first quarter 1993.

Stewart Appleberry announces recent award winners

Stewart Appleberry, Manufacturing and Engineering Manager, recently cited the Electronic Assembly Unit for increasing production output while maintaining minimum contract tolerance requirements. Alan Myers, Unit Supervisor, distributing certificates of merit at a luncheon in the unit's honor, noted, "This unit worked long hours under extreme pressure, sometimes nursing aging equipment, to deliver the required assemblies on time." Mr. Appleberry summed up the unit's contribution as ". . . the kind of personal sacrifice which will impact our ability to reduce costs and increase sales."

(continued)

Exhibit 3.2. (continued)

Robert Fisher named PDQ Salesman of the Year

Robert Fisher, Senior Account Executive from the Northeast Regional Sales Division, was selected *PDQ Salesman of the Year* for his outstanding contributions to increased product sales in consumer electronics. Mr. Fisher's creative sales approach "contributed significantly to increasing our market share during the recent recession," said John Smith, Northeast Regional Sales Manager.

Around the industry . . .

RQO, Inc., teaming with Samon Company, has been awarded the 55 million dollar contract for the commercial airline electronic standardization program. PDQ's design was eliminated from the competition in the first round evaluations earlier this year due to "lack of understanding of the requirements" reports Charles Burns, Business Development Manager.

Tamac, Co. beat PDQ on cost to win a contract with Virginia Power and Light to upgrade and manage their nuclear power plants.

General Electronics, Inc. announced the introduction of an advanced video disc player which will compete directly with PDQ's *Video-Disc* product line. Edward Sokol, Manager, Consumer Electronics, expects the new product to "capture the imagination of the public and a major market share. PDQ must devote more resources to advertising and marketing if we wish to compete in this arena."

PDQ benefits update

The recently negotiated contract with Local 121 resulted in a number of changes to the PDQ benefits package. Employees will be contributing a larger percentage of the cost of medical, life and accident insurance through payroll deductions. Formerly, PDQ paid the entire cost but increasing costs "must be shared between the employee and the company in order to improve the bottom line," said Thomas Jackson, Employee Relations Manager. Weekly deductions will begin in July.

In addition, all employees will contribute 3.5% of their gross salary to the pension fund on all income earned. Previously, PDQ paid the 3.5% contribution on the first $25,000 earned.

Around the company . . .

Susan Appleberry, daughter of Stewart Appleberry, Manufacturing and Engineering Manager, will attend the University of Pennsylvania, majoring in civil engineering in the fall. Susan, a straight A student, is president of her class, a varsity tennis player, champion chess master and co-chair of her high school science club. Susan's father says, "She's a very special person and her mother and I are very proud."

New Employees:

Allen Howard—*VideoDisc* Product Sales
Michael Bell—Junior Engineer
John Evans—Draftsman
Ann Reilly—Administrative Assistant

Recent promotions:

Tony Dale—Supervising Engineer
Roselyn Smith—Advertising Coordinator
Grant Welsh—Mid-West Regional Sales Manager

Service anniversaries:

Bob Bell—30 years
Betty Appleberry—25 years
Paul Katz—25 years

(continued)

Exhibit 3.2. (continued)

Tony Dale—20 years
Pamela Bolt—20 years
Meg Evans—10 years
James Hunter—10 years
Jim Fisher—10 years
Robert Appleberry, Jr.—10 years
Robert Murphy—5 years

Employee picnic planned

The employee picnic will be held on Saturday, July 12 at Rumpole Park from noon to dusk. Rain date is July 19th.

Reminders

Employees are reminded that first shift begins promptly at 7:30 a.m. and ends at 4:15 p.m. Lunch is from 12:00–12:45 p.m. All employees are expected to work normal shift hours unless permission has been given for alternative hours in advance by the manager.

PDQ buildings will ban smoking on the grounds beginning July 1, 1992. Smoking has been restricted in all indoor facilities since January, 1991. Carol Sparks, Accountant, cites rising health rates as the primary reasons for this restriction.

Quarterly sales winners will be announced in next week's **PDQ News**. This quarter's prize is an all expense paid trip for 2 to Hawaii.

Exhibit 3.3. The TNT Company Quiz

The TNT Company Quiz

1. Circle the adjectives that best characterize the organization's structure. Feel free to add any other observations you have.

a.	Centralized	Decentralized	Cannot tell
b.	Multi-layered	Flat	Cannot tell
c.	Complex	Simple	Cannot tell
d.	Product oriented	Function oriented	Cannot tell
e.	Local/Regional	National/International	Cannot tell

2. What four adjectives best describe the values and philosophy of the company?

   a. ______________________ c. ______________________

   b. ______________________ d. ______________________

3. Briefly describe the business outlook for the company and the business strategy being used.

   ____

   ____

4. How much interaction would you have with your immediate manager? Daily, weekly, monthly?

   ____

5. What is the probability that you would work in a team?

   ____

6. How much visibility would your work have to upper management?

   ____

7. Do you perceive any obstacles to your advancement in this company?

   ____

(continued)

Exhibit 3.3. (continued)

8. Do you think this organization requires narrow specialization or "jack-of-all-trade" skills?

____

9. Is engineering part of the mainstream of the business? Are you more or less likely to be a candidate for a layoff if you work in engineering?

____

10. What additional information would you like to find out? How would you go about doing this?

____

____

____

____

Exhibit 3.4. The PDQ Company Quiz

The PDQ Company Quiz

1. Circle the adjectives that best characterize the organization's structure. Feel free to add any other observations you have.

a.	Centralized	Decentralized	Cannot tell
b.	Multi-layered	Flat	Cannot tell
c.	Complex	Simple	Cannot tell
d.	Product oriented	Function oriented	Cannot tell
e.	Local/Regional	National/International	Cannot tell

2. What four adjectives best describe the values and philosophy of the company?

   a. ______________________ c. ______________________

   b. ______________________ d. ______________________

3. Briefly describe the business outlook for the company and the business strategy being used.

   ____

   ____

4. How much interaction would you have with your immediate manager? Daily, weekly, monthly?

   ____

5. What is the probability that you would work in a team?

   ____

6. How much visibility would your work have to upper management?

   ____

7. Do you perceive any obstacles to your advancement in this company?

   ____

(continued)

Exhibit 3.4. (continued)

8. Do you think this organization requires narrow specialization or ''jack-of-all-trade'' skills?

   ____

9. Is engineering part of the mainstream of the business? Are you more or less likely to be a candidate for a layoff if you work in engineering?

   ____

10. What additional information would you like to find out? How would you go about doing this?

    ____

    ____

    ____

    ____

Exhibit 3.5. Answers to Company Quizzes

Answers to Company Quizzes

TNT answers

Organization:
- Centralized
- Flat
- Simple (Matrix problems may make it complex)
- Function oriented
- National/International

Values and Philosophy:
- Quality, research and development
- Teamwork
- Delayering
- Outsourcing
- Health minded
- Culturally diverse
- No glass ceiling
- Employee oriented
- Family oriented
- Generous recognition for individual contributions to goals

Contact with Manager:
- Weekly/Monthly

Probability of Teamwork:
- High

Visibility to upper management:
- Likely

Obstacles to advancement:
- Business climate

Other:
Jack-of-all-trades orientation.
Engineering in the mainstream—layoffs on Video-Disc possible, but not probable.

PDQ answers

Organization:
- Decentralized
- Hierarchical
- Complex
- Product oriented
- Local/Regional

Values and Philosophy:
- Sales, marketing, advertising
- Patriarchical
- Family business/nepotism
- Outsourcing
- Cost minded
- Culturally homogeneous
- Glass ceiling
- Profit oriented
- Generous recognition for selected sales representatives' contributions to goals; minimal for others (for instance, shop floor workers)

Contact with Manager:
- Daily/Weekly

Probability of Teamwork:
- Low

Visibility to upper management:
- Unlikely

Obstacles to advancement:
- Business climate
- Glass ceiling
- Cultural differences
- Sales orientation
- Family business

Other:
Specialization valued.
Engineering integrated with product lines—layoffs on Video-Disc probable.

Benefits of Learning the Company's Values and Goals

How is a new employee affected by knowing or not knowing the company goals? Surely an entry-level employee cannot influence such high-level policies. True: It is not *your* influence on them but *their* influence on you and your performance that is important. Knowing where the company is going and how it intends to get there will help you understand decisions that are made at your level of the organization.

For example, suppose the supervisor who hired you said that the company sends new employees to extensive, off-site vendor training courses. Instead, you receive training by company representatives at the local site. You may feel cheated or duped, which can lead to frustration or doubts about your new employer. If, however, you have read that the company wants to build a strong internal training organization or that return on sales has not met expectations this year, you can interpret the training arrangements differently. Rather than taking the change personally, you will be able to understand it in the context of the organization's goals and current business situation. Similarly, if many of your tasks involve customer service and the company's objectives for the year include increasing customer satisfaction by 20 percent, you can use this information as a clue to what your supervisor will consider important when evaluating your performance. Giving top priority to customers could result in your receiving a higher performance rating.

Learning the Organization's Structure

Another key to understanding your organization's culture is the organization charts. Organization charts are pyramid-shaped box diagrams showing the superior–subordinate relationships and interactions of the chain of command. If the company is small, the entire reporting structure will fit on one page and can be quickly deciphered. Larger companies' charts may require many pages and will take longer to sort out. Study the organization charts to learn what function each unit performs, who reports to whom, where to go for help, and where to communicate various types of information. The following steps will help you navigate through the company structure:

1. Begin by focusing on the structure and role of your immediate unit and your function in the unit. Expand your research to the units with which you directly interact.

2. Fill in all the information you have gathered from coworkers and company publications. The following chart (**Exhibit 3.6** Learning the Organization Structure) explains the kinds of information you need to gather.

3. Next, prepare specific questions you still need answered. Discuss what you have found out about the organization with your supervisor and have your questions answered. Focus on how your job function relates to others in the organization and supports the objectives of the business. What you learn from this discussion will help you communicate appropriately with the people affected by your work, thus quickly gaining you their respect. You will also be displaying your understanding of the bigger picture—a characteristic that business values.

4. Continue with your research, filling in the blanks and expanding outward from your unit, until you understand the structure and function of the entire company.

5. At a later date, schedule a follow-up meeting with your supervisor to further discuss what you have learned about the entire company.

Exhibit 3.6. Learning the Organization Structure

Learning the Organization Structure

How is the organization defined?	By function? (That is, a marketing organization, an operations organization, a personnel department, and so forth.) By product? (That is, by product line or project with functional components underneath which belong strictly to that product or project.) As a matrix? (In matrix organizations, home units "lend" their employees to projects or product lines to work on specific assignments. When the assignment is over, the employee returns to the home unit and works there while awaiting the next assignment.) By region? (That is, by regional differences, with either functions, products, or a matrix underneath.)
What is the function of each unit?	The function of a unit includes its purpose, scope, and major tasks and responsibilities. It defines the authority, responsibility, and accountability of the supervisor of the unit. You cannot rely on the title of an organization for this information because sometimes the title is unclear or misleading. For instance, a unit called *Business Contracts and Advanced Processes* may leave you without a clue to its real function. Determine the specific tasks and responsibilities of each unit. Knowing which unit performs which functions will help you understand how your unit's function and your work relate to that of other units.
How many subordinates report directly to each superior?	This number is sometimes called "the span of control" for each unit supervisor and can be an indicator of the degree of job specialization or organizational complexity. It also tells you how much personal attention you can expect from your supervisor. The more people who report to your supervisor, the less time your supervisor can spend helping, advising, or training you and the more initiative you will have to assert on the job.

(continued)

Exhibit 3.6. (continued)

Who manages each unit and who reports to each supervisor?	Names are sometimes provided on organization charts, even down to the individual employee level. This will make your job very easy. You just have to check the date the chart was created and make any recent changes. If no names are given, you will have to gather this level of information yourself. Secretaries usually can help you find out who reports to whom. By learning the names of the people associated with each unit, you can learn their general duties by referring to the unit's function. You can use the organization charts as a memory jogger for names and functions of people you have met or heard about. The charts can also be a starting place when you need to find someone to help you.
How is work accomplished—in well-defined units with clear charters or in self-directed work teams?	Until recently, most companies were organized in well-defined hierarchies, similar to the organization structure of the U.S. military. Each unit and department had a clearly defined charter, or purpose, and no other unit could perform work covered by that charter. Each level of management had clearly stated approval authority. Often in this structure, release of a product or changes in policies or procedures required several levels of management approval. A new approach to getting work done is the creation of self-directed teams whose membership depends on the purpose of the team. These teams are *empowered* to define their own rules, select their own methods and procedures, and make decisions with minimal management intervention. Organizations normally will fall somewhere between these two extremes as more companies reorganize to achieve greater productivity at reduced costs. You must determine where your new organization falls on this continuum.

Creating Your Own Organization Chart

If your organization doesn't have formal organization charts, you can create your own from information in company publications and complete them by asking questions as we just discussed. **Exhibit 3.7** is an organization chart created just from the information in the TNT newsletter used in the company quizzes (**Exhibits 3.1** through **3.5**). Notice that there are no lines connecting the boxes yet. Without more information, it is hard to determine exactly who reports to whom. Some assumptions have been made based on the answers to the previous quizzes. The TNT organization chart would be:

- centralized (units report to a single supervisor who is responsible to the CEO)
- flat (few layers of management)
- simple (quality control would be under manufacturing, rather than report directly to the CEO)
- function oriented (engineering and manufacturing would play keys roles in the organization)
- reflecting a national/international approach.

Jobs that employees in the newsletter had held previously were added, as well as those that could be immediately identified.

The assumption is made that manufacturing is based on regions, while engineering is based on product line. By asking questions of your supervisor and coworkers, you can validate your assumptions and revise your own chart to reflect reality.

Exhibit 3.7. The TNT Organization Chart

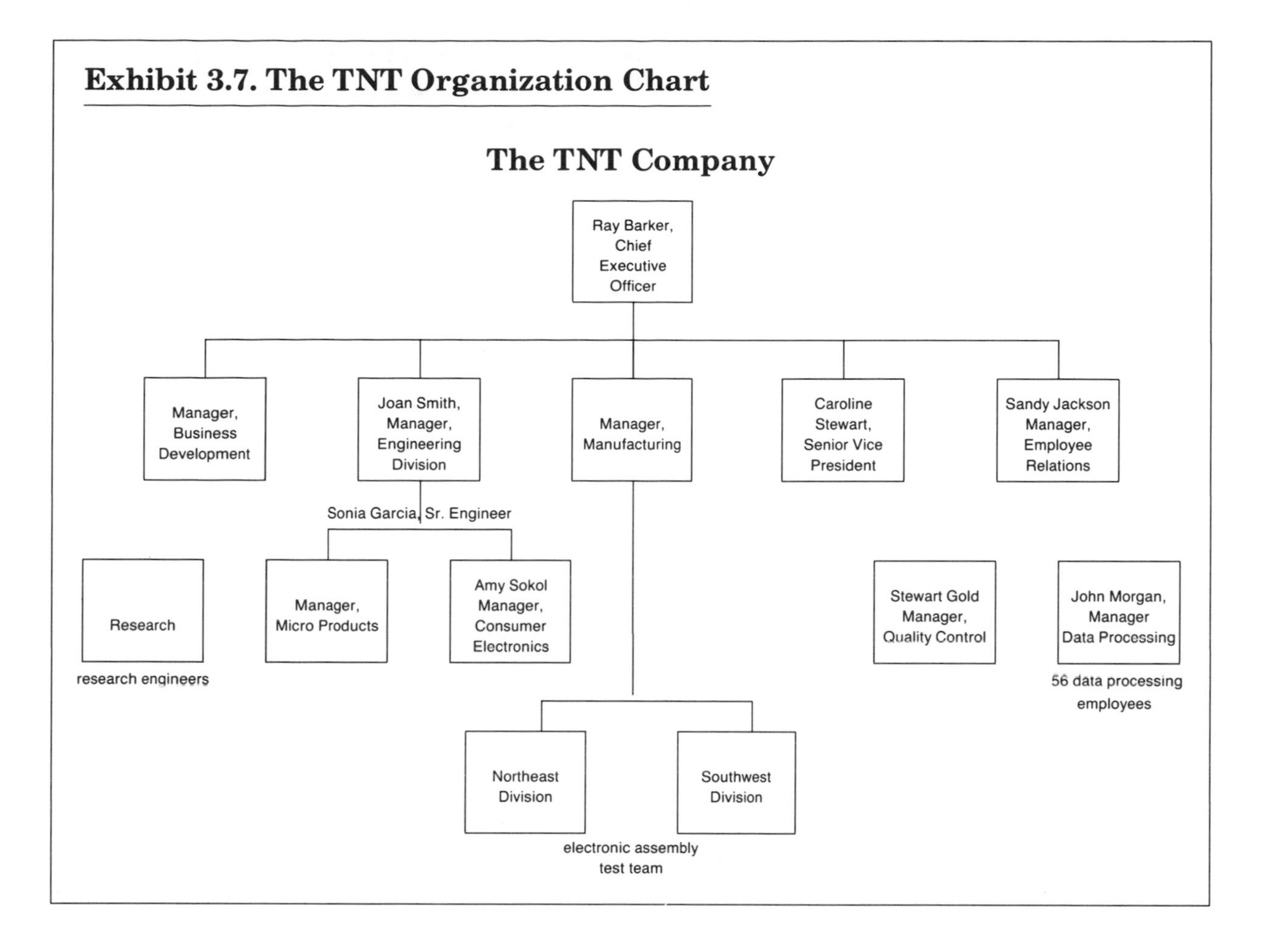

Benefits of Knowing Your Organization's Structure

One of the key benefits of understanding your unit and your role in it and the role and relationship of the other units in the company is that you can be productive very quickly. You will readily know where to go for help, where to communicate various types of information, how your work may be influencing that of others, and vice versa. Another benefit of knowing your organization's structure is that you may save yourself the embarrassment of not recognizing the name or face of a key figure within the company. Imagine the impression made by a recent hire who, when introduced by name only to the president of her firm at a company picnic asked, "What do you do for a living?"

Learning the Signs and Perks of Seniority

When you understand your unit and your role in it, learn the standard perquisites, or *perks,* that are associated with seniority and higher levels in the organizational hierarchy. For instance, seniority may warrant a reserved parking space or an invitation to an annual management trip to the Bahamas. Since perks are a subtle aspect of organizational culture, few people feel comfortable discussing them directly. This is information you may have to derive for yourself. Start by asking the employee relations representative or your supervisor to explain the general pay or "level" structure and associated titles that dictate the relative standing of individuals who are not supervisors. After you have identified the senior individuals by title, note the perks—such as private or larger work areas—enjoyed by them.

Benefits of Learning the Signs of Seniority

Once you can identify the senior employees in your company, you have simultaneously developed the ability to identify the probable experts in your workplace who can help you in performing your job. When you seek their assistance, make sure you know the unspoken rules on how to approach these people without becoming a nuisance.

Learning the signs of seniority will also provide clues to proper office behavior to how you will be treated. If you are a recent graduate at entry level, it is unlikely that you will have a private office with a window. Demanding, or even requesting, such an office will mark you as naive or worse—someone who has overestimated his or her role in the company.

Understanding Personnel Policies

Personnel policies cover a myriad of topics that represent the company's official stance on employee behavior. These policies probably will be available through your personnel department or from your supervisor. In smaller companies, personnel policies may be informal rather than written documents. You will have to ask your manager directly for this information. Specific personnel policies and procedures will guide you in understanding:

- the number of sick days you are allowed;
- policies governing other types of absences;
- the importance of arriving to work on time vs. flextime;
- formal procedures used to appraise your performance;
- your responsibilities when using company property, such as the telephone, reproduction and fax machines, or company credit cards.

Benefits of Learning Personnel Policies

Obey all personnel policies while you explore the more subtle aspects of your organization's culture. Individuals within your immediate unit may impose their own interpretation on company policy. However, do not violate written rules until you are sure which ones you can disregard with no negative consequences. Unless you understand exactly what the limits are, you may put your job in jeopardy over a simple long-distance phone call. This doesn't usually occur to new employees. Act cautiously, especially early on.

Accounting for Your Time

Another sensitive area regulated by company policy is accounting for your time. Every company expects you to work the number of hours you agreed to. Coming in late, taking long lunches, and leaving early violates this agreement. This is a particularly sensitive area for businesses with contracts. Contracts, especially government contracts, are strictly regulated.

You may have read about companies involved in serious law suits with the government over time charges. If you work on a contract, you must accurately record both your time and any expense accounts related to the contract. This is beyond a moral issue; it is imperative to your survival on the job.

Using Technical Procedures and Standards

Other policies that can affect your performance are technical procedures and standards. They are used as criteria for quality and productivity. Just as you had to ask for more general office documents, you may have to ask for copies of technical procedures and standards. Depending on the size of the company and the type of work you do, they will be more or less formal.

Benefits of Adhering to Procedures and Standards

Understand and follow technical procedures during your first months on the job. Even if coworkers ignore them, adhere to technical policies because you will improve your knowledge of your job. You really cannot judge which procedures to follow and which to ignore before you thoroughly understand them. Later on, after some experience, you can implement some of the suggestions in Chapter 5, "Performing Your Job," to improve or change procedures and standards related to your job.

Techniques for Learning the Ground Rules

Asking Questions

As a new employee, you are expected to ask many questions. Take advantage of this expectation. You need to learn everything from how to run the fax machine to what behavior will get you fired fastest. Early on, asking for explanations during a formal meeting will be tolerated, as long as you don't overdo it. Casual conversations can supply you with valuable information on who is who, what various organizations do, and what's hot on the office grapevine. This kind of information supplements all the written material you have discovered and what your supervisor told you.

When asking coworkers for information or assistance, never lose sight of the fact that your primary goal is to become self-reliant. One of the biggest mistakes new employees make is continuing to rely on coworkers for information they have asked for previously. Coworkers will continue to answer your questions if they are not the same ones repeatedly. To avoid this, do not depend on your memory alone. You will forget the number of the computer repair hot line as soon as you dial it. Instead, get in the habit of writing down the answers to your questions.

Keeping a Log Book

Keep a log book or organizer to help you organize the vast amount of information you are gathering. This is a common practice in the workplace among successful people and will help, not hinder, your productivity. You will find throughout this book many specific situations where we advise you to take notes. Keep your log with you throughout the day and record notes directly in a specific section. Take the time to review the log at the end of every day, elaborating on what you have learned and noting any questions you may have for further clarification.

Advantages of a log book

A daily log book has many advantages over scattered notes or relying on your memory:

1. A bound book will preserve chronological order. A loose-leaf book will allow you to reorganize the material into meaningful categories. In either case, get in the habit of recording the date of each notation.
2. By recording your daily accomplishments, you will be amassing the information needed to provide status to your supervisor.
3. At performance appraisal time, you will be able to summarize specific achievements to your supervisor without having to rely on vague memories.

Recording Jargon and Acronyms

Jargon and acronyms are a way of life in every industry. Many people emerge reeling from their first meeting where the only recognizable words were "a" and "the." Set aside a section for listing all company acronyms and their meanings. (Such a list may already exist. Ask for it.) You will be at a disadvantage until you master the organization's language. Your best, and least embarrassing, source of definitions is informal discussions with your coworkers. After a while, this new language will make sense to you—really! But you must make an effort to learn it as quickly as possible.

Learning Who's Who

If you record the name, title or function, organization, location, and phone number of the people you deal with, you can use it to complete your understanding of the organization. Recording the topic and key points made by the person could prove useful in the future. You do not know how long it will be before you have to contact the person again. For example, recording whom you talked to when getting your phone installed could prove useful six months down the road when you move to a new desk and need the phone moved.

What the log book isn't

Your work log is not a personal diary. It is merely a widely used personal tool for collecting supplementary information about your job. Do *not* use your log:

- to duplicate procedures documented elsewhere
- as a substitute for the office phone directory
- as a substitute for a project folder.

Your log should reflect a professional attitude. If you use a log book, the company could claim ownership of the contents because you wrote it on company time. If you need to produce documentation concerning a work problem, others may read your log. Keep this in mind.

Alternative to the log

As you become more experienced, keeping an extensive log book may no longer be necessary. Instead, use your appointment book as a shorter version of a log. Record the time, location, and topic for both formal and informal meetings. Make a note if a meeting is canceled or rescheduled. This will help you document problems beyond your control. If you cannot attend a meeting, record why you had to miss it. Also include all task due dates and whether or not you met them.

Expanding the Horizon: Stated Policies Versus Your Reality

You now have a fairly complete understanding of the formal definition of your organization's culture. The final step in fully understanding the culture is to validate what you have found against the reality you experience daily. Contrast your observations and personal experiences with the official policies. Keep exploring areas that are inconsistent until you're sure which policies and procedures you don't have to follow. Use socializing as an opportunity to expand your knowledge of coworkers and the organization. Until you really understand the culture, however, be wary of people who express only negative attitudes toward the company. Some disgruntled employees love to recruit new people to their "anti-establishment" cause. Listen to what everyone has to say but form your own judgment and opinions.

Reconciling with Reality

Determining how your immediate supervisor interprets the rules requires careful and repeated observation. For the first several months, conform to the defined procedures completely until it is clear what rules you can bend. For instance, many companies have what appear to be strict start and stop times for all employees. Some supervisors may feel this is not an appropriate rule for salaried professionals. You may see others coming and going as they please. Your supervisor, on the other hand, may be someone who abides by every company regulation and will call you on the carpet if you start arriving late. Know where your boss stands on the rules.

Summary

Understanding the organizational culture is not part of some "game." It is vital to your survival. Learning the culture of the workplace requires initiative and effort. By following these orientation techniques, you will understand the context in which you must perform your job. This understanding results in a smoother transition for the new employee, better performance appraisals, and improved visibility in the organization. Moreover, the more clearly you understand how the organization works, the more effectively you will be able to perform your own assignments.

Understanding Your Assignment

Introduction

Your performance on your first assignment sets the stage for the way your manager and teammates perceive you for as long as a year. It may determine how much (or how little) responsibility you receive once you've completed the task. It could influence the size of the raise you receive later in the year, or whether you receive one at all. If you are involved in a company restructuring or downsizing, it can even determine whether you keep your job or are laid off. Managers usually understand that new employees have much to learn and will make several mistakes along the way. Teammates remember being new on the job themselves. Nevertheless, you want to do the best you can in order to create a positive impression with both your manager and your coworkers.

Receiving a New Assignment

One of the biggest hurdles new employees face on their first assignment is figuring out what the task is and how to do it! Some sit paralyzed at their desks for days or even weeks, uncertain how to begin, yet afraid to ask questions. Often the reason new employees do not plunge into their work is that they are timid about asking for help and appearing incompetent. Managers and coworkers may get the impression that the employee is unmotivated and lazy.

Learning the mechanics of accepting an assignment will free you to focus on getting the task done. Applying the mechanics will stop new-assignment paralysis. Waiting to start a new assignment until you are comfortable with the definition of the task, the resources you will need, and how to locate the resources will help you avoid false starts or dead-end approaches.

Here is a sample conversation between a manager and a new employee that illustrates how many managers initiate new assignments. Assignments initiated by teams of coworkers may also follow this pattern.

MANAGER: Hi, Barbara. How are things going? Are you settling in here at TNT Corporation?

EMPLOYEE: Yes, I'm starting to find my way around.

MANAGER: Good. Let me know if you have any difficulties. The reason I wanted to talk to you today is that I have an assignment for you. We just put new IBM PCs on all the managers' desks. None of them have the time to evaluate the best spreadsheet for us to buy, so I'd like you to be responsible for that. Are you knowledgeable about spreadsheets that are on the market these days?

EMPLOYEE: I've used spreadsheets before, but I don't know a lot about all the products that are currently available.

MANAGER: Not to worry! There are lots of sources of information around—trade journals, anything else that comes to mind. . . . Come to think of it, Bill in manufacturing did a product evaluation for his department several months ago. He might be able to help you.

EMPLOYEE: Sounds good. When would you like this done by?

MANAGER: Oh, there's no rush. . . . Keep me posted and let me know if you have any questions.

Based on the discussion, what does Barbara know about her new assignment?

Why. The office just bought new computers for the managers to use. The managers don't have time to evaluate the best spreadsheet package they should buy, so this assignment has been given to the employee.

What. Barbara is to evaluate the available spreadsheets on the market and recommend which the department should buy.

How. Barbara can look at trade journals or any other things that come to mind.

Who. Bill in the manufacturing department made a similar evaluation for his department six months ago. He might be able to provide some help.

Where. Nothing was provided.

When. No rush.

But what potentially key information did the manager *not* tell Barbara?

Why. Barbara *doesn't know* how this assignment relates to the objectives of the office or to work that other people are doing. Therefore, she *doesn't know* if this is busywork to test her analytical skills, **or** if it has been mandated by a senior manager so that financial data can be shared electronically, **or** requested by a customer so financial data can be easily analyzed, **or** just because the department has extra spending money they can use on a luxury item.

What. Barbara *doesn't know* if the outcome of the assignment is to be a study report, an informal discussion with the manager, or whether she should just go out and buy the product she thinks best.

How. She *doesn't know* if she is supposed to contact the managers with the new PCs for their requirements for the new spreadsheet. She *doesn't know* if there is a process for performing cost–benefit analysis in this organization or if one is required. She *doesn't know* if there are specified vendor catalogues for her to use that limit the selection of the spreadsheet. She *doesn't know* if there are budget limitations that must be followed. She *doesn't know* if standards/requirements exist regarding capabilities that must be provided by the spreadsheet, or if it must fit with an existing tool set already on the computers.

Who. Barbara *doesn't know* if the recommendation is to be made to her supervisor, or the set of managers who will be using the tool, or a higher-level manager who may have required this work. She *doesn't know* if others in the office are evaluating other tools—if so, collaboration might get a good discount with one vendor. She *doesn't know* Bill's last name—there could be many "Bills" in manufacturing. She *doesn't know* if there is a purchasing or finance person or a customer she needs to coordinate with. She *doesn't know* if there are any experts in the department—is Bill the expert or are there others?

Where. If there is a requirement for specific vendor catalogues to use, Barbara *doesn't know* where they are. If the company has a specific way of performing cost–benefit analysis, she *doesn't know* where to find procedures for this type of analysis or previous examples she can follow.

When. Barbara *doesn't know* if "no rush" means by the end of the week or the end of the month. Perhaps the assignment is due whenever she gets to it because other tasks have a higher priority.

There's a lot more Barbara *doesn't* know about her new assignment than she *does* know!

Asking the Right Questions

The first step in developing the skill of receiving a new assignment is to learn the right questions to ask. Use the well-known reporter's questions (who, what, when, where, how, and why) as the ones to ask. At the end of your first meeting with your manager or team, you must either have the answers to all the questions that apply to the assignment or know where you can find the answers. Knowing the purpose of each question is the key to its effective use.

Why *are you being assigned the work?*

The answer to the first question may seem obvious: because it needs to be done! The purpose of the question, however, is to find out how the task fits into the overall goals of the organization and the ultimate effect of the assignment on those goals. Knowing the scope of the assignment will help you to determine how to plan and accomplish the task. It will also help you decide what parts of the assignment to spend the most time on if you have limited time and need to set priorities.

What *are you being asked to do?*

This question is likely to result in an incomplete answer because your manager or teammates may have unrealistic assumptions about what you already know. Make sure you learn what the *product* of your assignment is to be—a draft document, a prototype piece of software, a presentation—so you know *exactly* what is expected.

How *should you accomplish the task?*

The response to this question may be specific information or the name of a contact who can provide it. Be sensitive to the fact that managers do not always know every detail about how assignments are accomplished. Be content with the name of an expert resource. If working in a self-directed team, determining how to accomplish the task may be part of the assignment. Rely on your teammates for help in this area.

Every work environment evolves its own way of doing things. How you perform an assignment may be dictated by documented standards and procedures. If your organization does not have written standards and procedures, your task will be a little harder. Ask to see an example of a product from a similar assignment. Ask if it is an example of expected quality. If it isn't, ask how could it be improved.

If the assignment is complex enough, you may be expected to create a project plan. Ask if you need a plan. If you do, ask when you can get together with your manager to review it. For more information on how to develop a project plan see Chapter 5, "Performing Your Job."

Who *is involved with this task?*

You may already know the answer to this question from the answers to the previous questions. Are you part of a team? Do you need information from someone working on a related task? If you work in a large organization, get the full name of anyone involved. You will spend inordinate amounts of time tracking down "John in production" unless you insist on complete information.

Where *are any required resources located?*

If you know where required resources are located and how to access them, you will save time tracking them down. Resources include the materials, people, and knowledge you will need to accomplish the task. Are the standards you need located in a specific manual? Is there a library or database of historical data you need to perform an analysis? Do you need special equipment? Is the equipment located in a specific room for common use or is acquiring it part of your task? Do you have to do anything to gain access to the resources, such as obtain a key to a storeroom or a computer access code from someone? If you need to talk to an expert, do you know where you can find him or her?

When *is the assignment due?*

Imagine how Barbara would feel if she assumed that "no rush" meant she had several weeks to do the work and her manager came looking for the results in several days. You can avoid surprise due dates. Ask *exactly* when you must complete the assignment. Ask how to make a status report and how often you should do it on this particular assignment. If you know the task due date and whether interim milestones must be scheduled, you can plan your work better. You can also keep coworkers from being unprepared if they need the results of your task to begin theirs.

Using the Assignment Checklist

Now that you understand the basic questions to ask, use the following "Worksheet for New Assignments" to prepare more detailed questions tailored to your work environment. The "New Assignment Checklist," which follows the worksheet, shows many of the questions you need to ask. When receiving an assignment, however, you may have to think of other appropriate questions on the spot. As you become more familiar with the checklist through repeated use, you will no longer need it. You will completely understand how to ask: *why, what, how, who, where, and when.*

Worksheet for New Assignments

Why is this work being assigned?	
What are you being asked to do?	
How are you to accomplish the task?	
Who is involved with this task?	
Where are any required resources located?	
When is the assignment due?	

New Assignment Checklist

Why is this work being assigned?	What are the objectives of the task? How does this assignment relate to the objectives of the organization? How does this assignment relate to work other people are doing?
What are you being asked to do?	What is the expected outcome? To what degree of completion (draft, final product) is the work to be done? What is the outcome of the task to look like? Are results to be reported in the form of a paper? An informal status discussion with your manager? A formal presentation?
How are you to accomplish the task?	Are there defined procedures you must be following? Are there existing tools you can or should be using to do this work? Do standards exist for the format of the outcome? Is there an example you can follow of a similar outcome? Is a project plan warranted or expected?
Who else is involved in this task?	Who is the ultimate audience for the outcome? Are you supposed to work on this with any other individuals or teams? Who are the "experts" who can help you if you have questions? Who has done similar work whom you can talk to? Is there someone outside your immediate organization you should be coordinating with? Will any customers be involved? If so, is there anything you should know about them before you contact them?
Where are any required resources located?	Where are the resources (including people) located? Do you have to do anything to gain access to the resources?
When is the assignment due?	When exactly is the assignment to be completed? Are there any interim tasks that are due before the final product?

Discussing the Details of an Assignment

Your manager may set up an appointment to assign you a new task, stop by your work area, or catch you in the hall. You may be part of a team deciding what the assignment should be. Here are some pointers to ensure that you make the most of any discussion.

1. *Prepare and ask the questions you need answered before starting the new task.*

If you have advance notice of the meeting, prepare your questions using the "Worksheet for New Assignments." Don't be afraid to reference the "New Assignment Checklist" during the discussion to ensure you have covered all the points. Your advance preparation will leave a good impression with your manager or teammates.

If you don't have time to prepare the "New Assignment Checklist," remember "*why, what, how, who, where, and when.*" Make sure you have the specific answers you need before the conversation ends.

After the initial discussion, especially if you didn't have time to prepare your checklist, you may discover other questions you need answered. Don't hesitate to ask your manager or the experts these additional questions. To avoid bothering them with repeated questions, prepare all the questions and ask them at the same time. You don't always have to arrange a formal meeting to get your answers. See Chapter 7, "Communicating Effectively," for alternative ways of communicating with them.

2. *If your manager or teammates can't answer the questions, find out where you can get the answers.*

Many managers do not know the details of how tasks are accomplished in their organization. This is particularly true if the manager oversees many people who are performing very complex technical or diverse tasks. If this is the case, find out if there are others in the organization who can help you. Managers often assign new employees an experienced coach or "buddy." The buddy is responsible for showing you the ropes and answering your questions. If working on a team, your teammates are the source for this information.

3. *Take notes during the discussion.*

Don't be afraid to take extensive notes during the meeting. No one expects you to have a perfect memory. If you don't write down everything that your manager says, you may miss some important points. You may not realize this until you have been working on the assignment for some time. Some points you initially thought unimportant (and therefore ignored) may be extremely critical to your success on the task. You can use your detailed notes to avoid this problem.

4. *Summarize the assignment in your own words.*

During the discussion, summarize what you heard to make sure you understood. Even when two people are native English speakers, they can still interpret the same words differently. Don't accept jargon or acronyms unless you are sure you know what they mean. Repeating the task in your own words will probably result in additional clarification from your manager. Repeat the additional information. There may be even more to the task your manager has failed to explain.

5. *Set up a specific follow-up meeting to discuss your approach and progress.*

At the end of the initial discussion, arrange a time to get back together to go over your approach and progress. The purpose of this meeting is to make sure you really understand the task and are correctly working toward the solution. Be specific about the date and time for this meeting. If you accept a vague answer like "some time next week," chances are your manager's calendar will fill up and you won't be part of it. Teams should also set specific times for follow-up meetings.

Discuss what you will cover at the follow-up meeting and how formal it will be. The meeting will probably be an informal discussion of what you have accomplished up to that point. Ask how much you are expected to complete by the time of the follow-up meeting and take the work or status with you.

Conducting the Follow-Up Meeting

Not only is a follow-up meeting a chance to double-check that you are on track, it is also an opportunity to make a favorable impression on your manager or teammates. You want to prepare for this meeting as well. Here is a list of items to discuss at your follow-up meeting:

1. *Review what you have accomplished.*

Summarize your progress to this point. (Chapter 5 will give you some pointers on how to organize your work and measure your progress.) If you want some aspects of your work reviewed in greater detail, have those details available. Any materials you bring along should be neat and legible but not necessarily the quality expected of the finished product. Remember: You are making an impression! You do not want to show sloppy, unprofessional work. On the other hand, if you make the material perfect, your manager or teammates may wonder if you have too much time on your hands.

2. *State your assumptions.* If you made assumptions or decisions about the task, explain what they are and how you arrived at them. In the spreadsheet evaluation example, Barbara may have assumed that she should be contacting vendors for quotes. Some companies, to avoid legal complications, allow only the purchasing department to ask for quotes from vendors. If Barbara acts on her assumption without telling her manager, she may violate company policy. Stating your assumptions is a technique for confirming that you and your manager or teammates view the assignment the same way.

3. *Discuss what you have left to do.* Chapter 5 explains how to identify all the sub-tasks needed to complete your assignment. Tell your manager or teammates which sub-tasks are still incomplete. They need to understand what you think still needs to be done. If they disagree with your idea of the outcome, discuss what is really expected.

4. *Explain any concerns or problems that could interfere with completing the work.* Managers don't like surprises. Tell your manager if your task may not be completed as expected. You may be able to get your manager's or teammates' help in removing any barriers you have run into. For example, Barbara may not have received back issues of trade magazines from the company library. Her manager may know someone in the office who keeps back issues. Her problem is solved!

Every job has challenges that you are being paid to overcome. Be sure that any concerns and problems you discuss are ones you cannot personally fix. You do not want to appear to be whining. For example, a common challenge is that there never seems to be enough time to complete all the assigned work; don't complain to your manager that you have too much to do in too little time.

However, it may really be true that you don't have enough time to complete the task. If Barbara has one week to buy the new spreadsheet for the office, but it takes two weeks for the vendor to ship it, Barbara should discuss this problem. By identifying this real obstacle, Barbara might get her deadline extended, or she might find that she can go directly to a local computer store and buy the spreadsheet.

5. *Deal with feedback!* A final note on the follow-up meeting: You may receive feedback on your work during this meeting. Read Chapter 6, "Performance Feedback and Compensation," to make the most of this experience.

Expanding the Horizon: Understanding Your Position

Before we discuss how to understand your position, let's review the key points of this chapter:

1. **You** must establish a common understanding of your assignment with your manager or teammates, using the "New Assignment Checklist." A common understanding helps you to focus on doing what is expected. You will not waste time figuring out what to do or doing the wrong thing.

2. **You** must take the initiative to establish this common understanding by being prepared for these discussions so that they are effective.

3. **You** must communicate interim status to avoid surprises and make sure you are still on the right track.

Apply the Questions to Your Position

These very same principles apply to understanding the position that you were hired to fill. You must fully understand your manager's or teammates' expectations for your first year on the job. Since your position will probably consist of a variety of tasks and assignments, you can apply the same basic questions to this bigger picture:

- **Why** is my job important? How does it fit into the roles and responsibilities of this organization?

- **What** do they expect me to accomplish? Am I supposed to become a specialist in one area or accept responsibility for a variety of tasks?

- **How** am I to work? Do I have to master a set of procedures or standards before I am considered proficient in my work?

- **Who** will I be working with? Am I part of a team? Should I be working on my own?

- **Where** are the required resources (people, equipment, documentation) I need for my tasks?

- **When** should I be taking on greater responsibility? What rate of progress is expected?

Defining Performance Objectives for Your Position

Some companies will have a formal process for defining performance objectives that is strictly enforced. In this case, you will probably not have to take the initiative. Simply follow the company procedures and address the questions above during the discussion. You may have a tougher time if there is no formal process at your company. With or without a formal process, many managers and teams put day-to-day problems ahead of defining employees' performance objectives. No matter how difficult it is to get your manager or team to discuss your specific objectives with you, it is critical that you do so.

If there is no formal process, or a discussion with your team or manager has not been initiated by the end of your first month on the job, take the initiative—ask for such a discussion. During the discussion:

- Ask the questions (why . . . what . . . how . . . etc.) supplied above.
- Use the same techniques you used in efficiently receiving a new assignment.
- Translate the answers from your notes into performance objectives and supply a copy to your manager or teammates.
- Ask for a review of them to see if you have understood the expectations correctly.
- You and your manager or teammates should negotiate until you agree on these objectives.
- Revise the written objectives and supply a final version if there is no formal process to document the agreement.

The set of objectives becomes your "contract" for the next evaluation period. Have another discussion about halfway through the evaluation period to clarify any potential misunderstandings and incorporate any new tasks or assignments. If you don't establish clear objectives early in the evaluation period, you risk an unwelcome surprise at your first performance review.

Benefits of Performance Objectives

Richard, a friend of ours who is in sales, is a good example of someone who wished he had taken the initiative to establish performance objectives with his manager. Richard was excited when it came time for his review and salary discussion. He thought his salary increase would be substantial. He had been number one in sales of all the people who had been hired that year. Richard's customers liked him and he got along well with his boss. When it came time for the review, however, Richard received only an average rating and salary increase. Why?

Richard's manager explained that Richard's peers and the support personnel thought he was unfriendly because whenever he came into the office, he never stopped to talk to anyone. The people in the office were uncomfortable whenever he was around. They didn't think Richard was a team player. They thought him arrogant and unappreciative of the support the office staff provided for the sales staff. Despite all the wonderful things he had accomplished, Richard was rated as an average employee. Richard's reaction at the time: "Why didn't they tell me I'd be evaluated on that!" The question to Richard is "Why didn't you ask?"

Summary

Learning to ask the right questions leads to better understanding of your assignments and your overall responsibilities. If you use this skill, you will benefit in several ways. Starting with your very first assignment, you will be able to focus on completing the task rather than worrying about what the task entails and how to go about it. You will have a clearer understanding of what is expected and will be more receptive toward constructive feedback along the way. Finally, you will quickly be able to define with your manager or teammates the overall performance objectives you will be evaluated on, resulting in a better performance appraisal.

Performing Your Job

5

Introduction

Successful performance on the job depends on your natural abilities and attitudes towards work, your academic training and its relevance to the job, and your application of these characteristics to the tasks at hand. However, creativity, a positive attitude, and good grades are not enough. You must know how to plan your work, execute the plan, and communicate the results. To be truly successful, you must expand your job understanding from how to accomplish specifically assigned tasks to understanding how those tasks fit into the bigger picture of your company, how to improve upon the initial directions you are given, and how to increase the scope of your responsibilities. This chapter teaches the basic planning skills you need to accomplish specifically assigned tasks and explains how to grow from performing on the job to mastering your position.

Using Planning Techniques

Let's use an everyday experience to illustrate some planning techniques and their importance. Suppose you are called on a Saturday morning by the hostess for a surprise party that evening. She is in a pinch and asks you to please bake a birthday cake. You have made a few cakes for family and friends in the past and you don't want to let your friend down. Does your enthusiasm and experience guarantee success? Let's see.

Planning Step 1: Define the Assignment

The first step you need to follow, as described in Chapter 4, is to determine *what* you have been asked to do. You've learned the kinds of questions you need to ask your hostess to completely understand what you are agreeing to do. Use the "Worksheet for New Assignments" from Chapter 4 to determine the information you must have to begin your plan. **Exhibit 5.1** shows the worksheet filled in as if you were working on a job-related task.

Exhibit 5.1. Completed "Worksheet for New Assignments"

Why is this work being assigned?	The hostess of a surprise birthday party does not have time to perform the task herself with so many other preparations to make.
What are you being asked to do?	Bake a chocolate birthday cake, iced and decorated, which will serve 25 people.
How are you to accomplish the task?	The hostess would like the cake to be home baked, not bought, but does not care if you use a cake mix or bake it from a recipe.
Who is involved with this task?	You are on your own unless you can recruit a friend to help you. Your hostess doesn't care who else you involve as long as they can keep a secret.
Where are any required resources located?	You will have to determine what resources you need. The hostess cannot offer any resources, such as the use of her oven, to help you.
When is the assignment due?	The cake must be delivered to the hostess by 7 P.M. that evening so she can hide the cake before the guest of honor arrives.

Planning Step 2: Determining All the Tasks

The next step is to address *how* you will go about baking the cake. Breaking down an assignment into all its tasks and sub-tasks, defining each one and determining the order in which to proceed seems to be the hardest thing for new employees to do but it is a pivotal step in planning your work. There are several techniques that can help you break down the overall assignment into the major tasks:

1. You can start at the beginning and list tasks as they occur in sequence to produce the end product. This technique works well if you have some experience with a similar assignment.

2. You can start with the end product and work backwards. This technique keeps the required output foremost in your mind and helps you avoid overlooking necessary steps to producing it.

3. You can randomly think of the tasks then put them in the proper sequence. If you choose this approach, look over the list several times, letting each task suggest others and determining any missing tasks.

No one technique works better than another but people seem to have a natural preference for one over the others. Each will work alone but because each addresses the assignment from a different perspective, using all three, in whatever order you wish, will help ensure you have identified all the major tasks.

1. *Define the initial task list.*

Because you have some experience in baking cakes, you start at the beginning and come up with the following list of the major tasks to be accomplished. Notice that because task lists describe actions you must take, a verb is always used. Using action-oriented verbs forces you to specify exactly what has to be done, thus avoiding vaguely defined tasks.

1. Decide on mix or find recipe.
2. Gather ingredients.
3. Assemble baking equipment.
4. Mix and bake cake.
5. Ice cake.
6. Decorate cake.
7. Deliver cake.

2. *Review the initial task list focusing on the product.*

Next review the task list starting with the end product in mind. You can remember you're nearly out of gas so you add that sub-task. You know you often forget to preheat the oven so you add a "reminder" task. The new task list looks like the following list with the changes emphasized in bold print.

1. Decide on mix or find recipe.
2. Gather ingredients.
3. Assemble baking equipment.
   a. **Preheat oven.**
4. Mix and bake cake.
5. Ice cake.
6. Decorate cake.
7. Deliver cake.
   a. **Get gas in car.**
   b. **Check directions to party.**

3. *Review the list again, filling in forgotten steps.*

Finally review the task list and randomly write down other tasks as they occur to you. You remember you have to also shower and get dressed for the party, you have to allow time for the cake to cool, and so on. You add one missing major task and several sub-tasks:

1. Decide on mix or find recipe.
2. Gather ingredients.
   a. **Check pantry.**
   b. **Buy ingredients.**
3. Assemble baking equipment.
   a. Preheat oven.
4. Mix and bake cake.
5. **Cool cake.**
6. Ice cake.
7. Decorate cake.
8. Deliver cake.
   a. **Dress for party.**
   b. Get gas for car.
   c. Check directions to party.

4. *Order the tasks chronologically.*

Once you have the task list, put all tasks and sub-tasks in the order in which they must occur. Make a note of tasks which can be worked in parallel. This step identifies tasks and sub-tasks which can be broken down further, tasks which are in the wrong order and sometimes missing tasks or sub-tasks. Our new task list now looks like this:

1. Decide on mix or find recipe.
2. Gather ingredients.
   a. Check pantry.
   b. Make list of missing ingredients.
   c. Get gas for car. (order change)
   d. Buy ingredients.
3. Assemble baking equipment.
   a. Pre-heat oven.
4. Mix and bake cake.
5. Cool cake.
   a. Shower while cake is cooling. (new)
6. Ice cake.
7. Decorate cake.
8. **Dress for party** (order change)
9. **Check directions to party.** (order change)
10. **Deliver cake**. (order change)

You now have a well-thought-out list of tasks to accomplish in order to bake and deliver your cake on time. As you can see from the example, the plan evolved and improved through many iterations and refinements. Planning takes time, but in the long run it will result in a better product, improve your performance, and help you avoid pitfalls which can be identified ahead of time, such as running out of gas on the way to the grocery store!

Tips for On-the-Job Planning

When planning a real work assignment, include secondary tasks which may improve the quality of your performance or product. For example, identify appropriate places to give your supervisor interim status on your progress and list them. Identify draft products which can be reviewed by someone else to improve their quality, and list the review task. Determine if any of the tasks need to be performed by others and if you must provide input before they can start their tasks.

Planning Step 3: Schedule All the Tasks

Any task has a minimum, maximum, and average amount of time required to complete it. For example, depending on the time of day and which day of the week it is, it can take from five to fifteen minutes to complete the task of getting gas at your local gas station. If you get gas early Sunday morning, it may take only five minutes, but you must allot the time based on your need to get gas on Saturday before going to the grocery store.

1. *Estimate the amount of time for each task.*

The first step in developing a schedule is to allot an amount of time to each task and sub-task. Later we will address making the schedule fit the time allotted, so avoid this in the beginning. Just make reasonable estimates based on the circumstances you are aware of, using averages rather than minimums or maximums. Start with those tasks whose length is fairly well defined. Then make very generous estimates for those tasks you are unsure of. Notice that time can be allocated as a sum of sub-task times or listed separately. Just don't double count when summing the times (watch out for parallel tasks).

Task	Time	Total
1. Decide on mix or find recipe.	60 minutes (estimate)	60
2. Gather ingredients.	60 minutes (sum of sub-tasks)	60
a. Check pantry.	10 minutes	
b. Make list of missing ingredients.	10 minutes	
c. Get gas for car.	10 minutes	
d. Buy ingredients.	30 minutes	
3. Assemble baking equipment.	10 minutes	10
a. Preheat oven.	(Minor task included in 10 minutes)	
4. Mix and bake cake.	75 minutes	75
5. Cool cake.	45 minutes	45
a. Shower while cake is cooling.	15 minutes (parallel with task 5)	
6. Ice cake.	20 minutes	20
7. Decorate cake.	60 minutes (estimate—you've never done it before)	60
8. Dress for party.	30 minutes	30
9. Check directions to party.	5 minutes	5
10. Deliver cake.	30 minutes	30
	Total clock time	6 hrs., 35 min.

Many people think that working backwards when scheduling can help keep the end date in mind. The problem with this technique, at least when developing the initial schedule, is the tendency to force the tasks into the time frame you have been given, thus underestimating the time it will take you. Underestimating tasks is a common problem with most schedules.

2. *Determine if the task estimates fit the due date.*

Once you have developed the basic schedule, determine whether or not it fits in the given time frame for delivery of your product. For instance, in our example, if it is now 10 A.M., you have two "extra" or unallocated hours before 7 P.M. This is also called *slack time.* Since two of your major tasks, tasks 1 and 7, may be underestimated quite substantially, proceed to the next two steps immediately and complete your plan so you can get started on the work while maintaining your slack time to cover unforeseen circumstances. If it is now 12:30, you have *exactly* the amount of time you think it will take to complete your plan on time. You may still be at risk of failing to meet your deadline. Those estimated times may not be accurate and you may have to adjust the plan accordingly to meet your deadline. Complete the next two steps with this in mind, trying to bring in the schedule so you have some slack time. Finally, if you went back to bed for several hours after the initial phone call, it may now be 2 P.M. You are in trouble! Complete the next two steps where you will learn how to adjust a tight schedule or re-plan the tasks.

Planning Step 4: Identify Resources and Alternatives

1. *Identify all the resources you need to accomplish the tasks you identified.*

Resources include people, equipment, facilities, and documents. Determine if these resources need to be ordered or acquired in some other way. Add sub-tasks to arrange for all resources far enough in advance that they will be available when you need them. Add these tasks to your schedule.

2. *Determine if adding resources will help meet the schedule.*

Resources can also be added to a plan to help bring in a schedule to fit the time frame allotted. Sometimes tasks which you personally cannot perform in parallel can be given to others. Sometimes adding experienced resources (more experienced than you are) or considering alternatives can shorten the length of a task. In our example, does your mother or a friend already have a recipe for a chocolate cake which feeds 25? A quick phone call could reduce your schedule by almost an hour. Using a cake mix is another possibility. Using prefabricated cake decorations rather than creating decorations by hand could further reduce the schedule. You will have to factor some or all of these alternatives and resources into your plan if your current schedule has no slack or if you cannot currently meet the end date.

Planning Step 5: Evaluate Your Final Plan

1. *Identify the critical path.*

Identify the series of tasks that depend on each other for either their start or completion. This is called the *critical path* of the schedule. While other tasks may have slack time or can be done in parallel, the tasks on the critical path determine whether or not you will meet your deadline.

For instance, in the cake-baking example, task 2 cannot be started until task 1 is completed. Task 1 is on the critical path. Task 3 can be started but not completed until task 1 is completed. Task 3, however, can be done in parallel with tasks 2c and 2d, if you have the resources to send someone else out to get gas and buy ingredients. Below are the critical path tasks on our re-planned schedule.

Task	Time	Minutes
1. Use mix or call for recipe.	**5 minutes**	**5**
a. Arrange for friend to help.	5 minutes	5
2. Gather ingredients.	**60 minutes (sum of sub-tasks)**	**60**
a. Check pantry.	10 minutes	
b. Make list of missing ingredients.	10 minutes	
c. Get gas for car.	10 minutes—delegate to friend	
d. Buy ingredients.	30 minutes—delegate to friend	
3. Assemble baking equipment.	**10 minutes**	**10**
a. Preheat oven.	(Minor task included in 10 minutes)	
4. Mix and bake cake.	**75 minutes**	**75**
5. Cool cake.	**45 minutes**	**45**
a. Shower while cake is cooling.	15 minutes (parallel with task 5)	
6. Ice cake.	**20 minutes**	**20**
7. Decorate cake.	**15 minutes using prefabricated decorations**	**15**
8. Dress for party.	**30 minutes**	**30**
9. Check directions to party.	**5 minutes**	**5**
10. Deliver cake.	**30 minutes**	**30**
	Total clock time	5 hrs.

2. *Determine the completion date.*

The total length of time for tasks on the critical path determines the completion date. When trying to bring in your schedule or build in more slack time, concentrate on these tasks. When executing your plan, critical path tasks are the ones which must be closely monitored to ensure your success.

3. Verify that the schedule fits within the time frame.

Based on the critical path, the schedule now fits within the time frame, whether you are starting at 10 A.M., 12 noon, or 2 P.M.

4. Allow for contingencies.

If you stayed in bed after your early morning phone call and it is now 2 P.M., no slack time is available with the above plan. Using that friend to ice and decorate the cake, while you dress for the party, brings the schedule down another 30 minutes, enough to almost guarantee you will meet the end date, as shown below, allowing for some contingencies.

Task	Time	Minutes
1. Use mix or call for recipe.	**5 minutes**	**5**
a. Arrange for friend to help.	5 minutes	5
2. Gather ingredients.	**60 minutes (sum of sub-tasks)**	**60**
a. Check pantry.	10 minutes	
b. Make list of missing ingredients.	10 minutes	
c. Get gas for car.	10 minutes—delegate to friend	
d. Buy ingredients.	30 minutes—delegate to friend	
3. Assemble baking equipment.	**10 minutes**	**10**
a. Preheat oven.	(Minor task included in 10 minutes)	
4. Mix and bake cake.	**75 minutes**	**75**
5. Cool cake.	**45 minutes**	**45**
a. Shower while cake is cooling.	15 minutes (parallel with task 5)	
6. Ice cake.	**20 minutes—delegate to friend**	**20**
7. Decorate cake.	**15 minutes using prefabricated decorations—delegate to friend**	**15**
8. Dress for party.	30 minutes (parallel with tasks 6 and 7)	
9. Check directions to party.	**5 minutes**	**5**
10. Deliver cake.	**30 minutes**	**30**
	Total clock time	4 hrs., 30 min.

5. Determine the risk to the plan.

Depending on your circumstances, either of these plans should now work. However, you must consider the risks associated with the plans. The higher your dependency on the skill, availability, and commitment of a friend, the higher the risk to the quality of the product, although it appears to reduce the risk of missing your schedule. Since your original time estimates were based on how long it would take *you* to perform the tasks, you must now consider whether your friend can do the tasks in the time allotted.

Scheduling Risks in the Workplace

Other risks to consider in work plans include: the introduction of new technologies; costly alternatives to reduce the schedule while incurring costs that are too high for the budget; dependency on someone else's input, including suppliers; and something called the *learning curve* (the amount of time required for someone new to a task to come up to speed on it). Even experienced workers consistently underestimate the amount of time needed to learn how to accomplish a new task. When you are satisfied that you have done a good job of balancing schedule risk with these other types of risk, you are ready to review your plan with your supervisor.

Presenting Your Plan to Your Supervisor

In your first follow-up meeting with your supervisor, discuss what you have accomplished so far on the assignment. Present your project plan and indicate how you made your decisions concerning the plan. Make sure to discuss any assumptions you have made so your supervisor can evaluate whether or not they are valid assumptions on which to base your plan. Discuss what's left to do and any concerns you have identified during the planning phase. If your supervisor finds the risk factors of your plan too high, you may have to re-plan the assignment based on a new completion date the supervisor supplies or other information which alters your assumptions or judgments. Schedule another meeting with your supervisor if necessary. Later on, your project plans may not have to be reviewed by your supervisor. This is a function of how well your planning skills are developing and how important or visible the assignment is.

Schedule short, interim follow-up status meetings with your supervisor. In follow-up meetings, do not return to your supervisor and say the task cannot be done. It may not be feasible in the time frame allotted or it may require more resources or creative alternatives, but supervisors do not usually assign impossible tasks. Your job is to learn to plan and re-plan to take these things into consideration. Provide alternative solutions to your supervisor.

Following the Plan

If your plan is well thought out, performing the assignment will just be a matter of executing the tasks as you planned them. As you go forward, record on the plan which tasks are complete and how long they took. This can be useful information for improving your next project plan. Note ways to do things differently next time and watch for patterns where you consistently overestimated or underestimated certain types of tasks.

As mentioned earlier, a key to keeping on schedule is to monitor performance on critical path terms. If they are not completed on time, your plan is unlikely to be completed on schedule. At the first hint of trouble, re-plan the assignment and discuss it with your supervisor. Since supervisors do not like surprises, not only should you see your supervisor when the end date is in jeopardy, but also when obstacles you can't overcome have arisen or if you are going to miss an interim deadline someone else is depending on.

Re-Planning an Assignment

Many factors can affect a plan's execution. You may have forgotten a sub-task or two. Your estimates may not have allowed enough time for a learning curve or enough slack time. Your assumptions, even those agreed to by your supervisor, could be wrong, such as thinking a vendor will always deliver a product on time. Finally, the unexpected can occur. A key resource can get sick or be diverted to higher priority tasks. These setbacks do not necessarily make you a poor planner. Most are normal business occurrences and you will learn to anticipate them and plan for them as you gain more experience.

To perform a re-plan, follow the original five planning steps. At each step include the following:

1. **Determine what has changed and how it has changed.**
2. **Review how tasks and sub-tasks have changed. Add, modify, or delete tasks and sub-tasks, as needed.**
3. **Reschedule or reorder tasks, as needed.**
4. **Determine if additional resources or alternative solutions can be applied to the tasks.**
5. **Evaluate the re-plan for new risks.**

Review the changes with your supervisor if they require a change in the end date. Then follow the new plan to completion. Unfortunately, sometimes several re-planning sessions may be needed on complex assignments or those that run over a long period of time. This can be very frustrating, especially when you must take time away from actually doing the work in order to change your plan. You may be tempted to ignore re-planning in the heat of the moment. However, the benefits of planning far outweigh the time expended, and reworking your plan will ensure that you can meet your end date while producing a quality product.

Planning Multiple Assignments

The complexity of planning increases if you must perform several assignments at the same time. While each individual assignment plan may appear reasonable and feasible when reviewed on its own, when they are combined they can result in overloading your schedule or that of others involved in the assignments. Each individual plan must be coordinated with the others so that your time, and that of any other people involved, is reasonably allocated. Using a scheduling software package can ease the burden of this coordination. If you do not have access to one, however, lay out the plans against a calendar and determine how you can schedule tasks to smooth peaks and valleys in your time. You may have to put in some overtime occasionally to overcome unanticipated obstacles but *you should not include overtime when creating your plan.* Working extensive overtime over long periods of time will result in lower productivity and quality. In addition, you cannot schedule and count on others to do overtime to meet your plan. Plans should be based on a regular work day with overtime used as a means of recovering from unexpected problems. Planning, scheduling, and monitoring the progress of your work is a minimal requirement for performing your job at a satisfactory level. The remainder of this chapter discusses *mastery* of your job—moving beyond just an acceptable level of performance.

Expanding the Horizon: Mastering the Job

During a meeting to discuss a problem with a financial system, a financial analyst was unable to clearly explain what the problem was. As the group continued to probe, she finally said in frustration, "I don't have to know what I'm doing. I just have to do it." This statement illustrates one of the most serious myths an employee can harbor—that rote performance of the job is all that is required. To succeed, you must understand more than the *what* of your job; you must understand the *how* and *why* so you can participate in problem-solving and job-improvement activities.

During your first year on the job, you should be moving through various stages of job understanding. Each stage has a different emphasis and goal. Being aware of these stages will help you focus your learning energies appropriately. These stages are not lockstep. One stage often overlaps another. You may be in a different stage for each task you perform. These stages provide a way for you to evaluate your progress in mastering your job.

The Benefits of Mastering Your Job

The benefit to you of mastering your job is that you will improve your performance evaluation and learn many new skills to position yourself for further advancement. If you have joined a company that is moving to the concept of a self-directed work force, it may be imperative for you to progress quickly through the stages of mastery. The idea behind a self-directed work force is to place more decision-making power into the hands of the people closest to the work problems. Solutions to problems, as well as productivity and quality improvements, are now expected to come from and be implemented by the entire work force, not just the more senior employees and management.

Stage 1: Understanding WHAT to Do

The most elementary stage of your job mastery is understanding *what* is expected of you—the scope of your responsibilities and how to get them done. This stage has two steps to it.

1. *Determine all the tasks for which you have responsibility.*

The length of time this stage lasts depends on the type of work you have been hired to do. If your job involves the repetitive performance of a few well-defined tasks, such as determining if applicants are qualified for a mortgage, you will pass more quickly from this stage to the next than a person whose job involves less structured tasks.

2. *Learn the mechanics of your tasks.*

Certain mechanical processes are needed to perform your tasks; for example, following a set of procedures for responding to a health insurance claim or apply certain formulas to determine the orbit of a satellite. You may have to become proficient with certain "tools" associated with your job, such as a word processing package. Just like learning the basics in school, learning the basic mechanics of your assigned tasks is a prerequisite to moving on effectively to the next stages.

Stage 2: Understanding HOW Things Really Work

Knowing what to do is not the same as having an in-depth understanding of what goes on behind the scenes. The goal of the second stage of job mastery is to learn how your job tasks really get accomplished so you know what to do when events don't follow the mechanical process you learned in Stage 1.

1. *Learn how the solutions work.*

When you were in elementary school you first memorized that 5+6=11, and later learned the mathematical concept of base=10 addition. When you first learned to spell, you memorized the plural forms of many words, and later learned the rules for adding "s" to singular noun forms to form plurals. Similarly in your job, you must supplement the rote learning you did in Stage 1 with the theory behind the case. This is Stage 2. This more in-depth understanding will help you make sound decisions when something goes wrong, helping you to determine what alternative steps can be taken and when. Your sources for uncovering the *how* of your job include your coworkers, other available experts, and your supervisor. Though everyone is busy, most will usually respond favorably to a reasonable request for help. Don't waste their time—come prepared to any meetings you set up with well-thought-out questions and take notes. No one will appreciate having to answer the same questions over and over.

2. *Wean yourself from the experts.*

We have observed that one of the hardest things for a new employee to do is stop using coworkers and experts for a "quick fix" to a problem and to rely on one's self for answers. While the "quick fix" may be necessary to solve a crisis situation, unless the new employee takes the time to learn why and how the solution worked, he or she remains dependent on others—and stuck in the first stage of development. This situation is compounded by the fact that if coworkers and experts are especially busy, they will simply fix the problem for you. It is easier and faster to do this than to take the time to explain the solution to you. You will then be unable to help yourself the next time. If, after several months on the job, you find that you are relying on the experts more than once or twice a month, you need to evaluate just what is lacking in your knowledge and find a more efficient way to learn. Push yourself to learn! Reference material is one place to start. Have you really tried to fix your own problems with the help of the material? Have you spent time away from work trying to understand the material? Alternatively, does the company offer after-hour courses on the topic? Do you need to attend night school to learn more about the topic? Is formal training available? Investigate your options and take action! If necessary, seek assistance from your supervisor if company training dollars will be required for you to gain the additional knowledge you need.

Stage 3: Understanding the WHY of Your Job

We have observed that this third stage of mastering your job is the one that the most employees fail to reach. The goal of Stage 3 of mastering your job is to understand how the tasks assigned to you fit into the bigger whole of the organization. This is not particularly difficult to understand. Gaining this knowledge is usually just a question of taking the initiative to do so. We suggest you investigate the following areas.

1. *Why is your job important?*

Every company has a reason for the existence of every job within it. Companies cannot afford to pay people to do work that does not contribute to their goals and objectives. What is the primary reason for the existence of your job? Do you directly help to produce a product? Bring in new business? Perform marketable services? Or do you function in a support role—as an administrator, a facilities specialist, or in personnel? Knowing the reason for your job and how it contributes to the goals of your company will help you decide what aspects of your job you should spend the most time on. For example, if you have a marketing job responsible for winning new clients for your company, you would probably want to spend more time developing a network of contacts and meeting potential new customers than on developing an elaborate database in which to record information about them. Knowing how your job fits into the bigger company picture will also help you understand and be more accepting of various management decisions that affect your organization. A support role, for instance, is likely to receive less training dollars than a line job and, during difficult financial times, would be a more likely candidate for a layoff than would be a role that contributes directly to the company's bottom line. Return to Chapter 3 for tips on understanding your company's objectives and how you might contribute to them.

2. *Determine how your tasks relate to those of others.*

No employee works totally independently of the rest of the larger organization. What happens to the output of your tasks when you complete them? You can probably get a tangible answer to this question relatively easy. Less obvious are the ramifications of innocent actions you might take. If you request last minute weekend support from a secretary, will it require the company to pay time plus a premium to bring that person in? Does your need warrant that extra expenditure? Did you know that running a computer job all weekend long cost the company several thousand dollars of processing fees? Were they in the budget?

Once you are proficient at completing your tasks, take the time to thoroughly understand the impact of your actions on others. You will be a more appreciated employee if you are especially attentive to quality and timeliness when your work is input to others' tasks or when it significantly and visibly contributes to the company's objectives. Attention to the less obvious outcomes of your actions will avoid embarrassing consequences and gain you the reputation as a person who has taken the time to understand how your company works.

What to Do with This Knowledge

Once you understand the ins and outs of your job, you can and should begin to look for ways to improve it. If you do not fully understand your job, you may be jumping to conclusions about the ways to improve it. Continue to learn how things are done until you can explain the global ramifications on productivity or quality when making a change. Use the following steps when you're ready to make improvements.

1. *Determine if there are really good reasons for the way things are done or if they are just the "way it's always been."*

Areas to consider in this stage include whether there are unnecessary people in the communications loop, excessive paperwork, labor-intensive or repetitive tasks, periodic reports which go unread, or overly complex procedures to follow. You are searching for waste, redundancy, rework (fixing errors or defects), and inefficiency.

2. *Discover and confirm how to improve.*

What do the people in the communications loop really do with the information? Is the paper trail merely bureaucratic or is it used during the yearly audit? Can labor-intensive or repetitive tasks be eliminated or automated? Can the complex procedures be simplified without sacrificing quality or violating government or other regulations? You cannot just point to a problem, you must find a way to fix it. Now you probably must turn even more to yourself for the answer. If your coworkers are performing similar jobs, they have either not discovered the problem or they have no solution. If the problem is one which affects only you, you can try alternatives out until you have a workable solution. In all likelihood, others will be affected and you must get approval before proceeding. Be aware as you proceed, that what you are proposing is *change*, and change is often painful for the people involved and expensive, in the short run, for an organization. Resistance to change can manifest itself in many subtle ways.

3. *Determine the feasibility of the change.*

Before you present your ideas to your supervisor, you must be sure your solution is feasible and will result in real benefit to the organization. There are two basic aspects of feasibility to be considered. Technically (or administratively), can it be done? And how much will it cost?

Start your feasibility study by discussing your proposal with your coworkers. Evaluate their feedback carefully. Don't be discouraged unless they can show you technical reasons why your solution won't work and you confirm them with an expert or prove it to yourself. Vague objections couched in terms like "Management will never buy into that" or "I tried to get that changed three years ago; don't waste your breath" are excuses to avoid change. Do not be surprised if management is equally resistant to the change.

4. *Quantify your solution.*

Quantify as much as possible the time, money, or quality effects of the problem. For example, if the report you think should be eliminated averages 25 pages and is distributed to 100 people monthly, not only can you determine the number of pages wasted per year, think in terms of the cost to produce, distribute, and throw away the report (e.g., computer time, printing time, mail room time, secretary time, trash collection).

Balance the potential savings against the cost of the solution. If your solution involves eliminating something (e.g., the needless paperwork), you need to consider at least the effort required to notify everyone involved of the change. If the solution requires some additional work to effect the change (e.g., rewriting a procedure and retraining people), the best you can do is estimate what it would take. Estimate the time for tasks you are familiar with and consult with other people who would be involved in the change.

If the cost of the change seems high in relationship to the benefit, you may not have a viable solution. Calculate, or ask your supervisor to help you calculate, the return on investment. If $5,000 must be invested to implement the change, how long will it be before the company recoups the money?

5. *"Sell" your solution.* Now that you've done your homework, you're ready to take your idea to the people (coworkers or supervisor) required to agree to its implementation. Again, remember that most people are uncomfortable with change and are likely to resist it, especially if the change is great. Use the potential cost savings and solution-costs data you have collected to factually present your ideas. Be prepared for rejection. New ideas are often ignored initially. Listen to the objections. Try again to sell your idea later on (it may have to be days later), addressing the concerns voiced earlier. Alternatively, is there a way you can partially implement your idea in your own sphere of control so that you can demonstrate partial benefits? Finally, accept defeat if you risk making a pest of yourself.

If all this seems excessive, it may be. Usually the types of improvements you will be able to suggest in your first year on the job will not have significant impact on your company's bottom line. Don't underestimate yourself, through. Sometimes all it takes is a fresh point of view and a questioning mind to discover significant waste in a company.

Summary

This chapter gives you the skills to accomplish individual tasks and to master your position. The next chapter, Performance Feedback and Compensation, will provide the skills needed to learn and profit from the feedback you get on your performance. It also describes the types of recognition or compensation you may receive for your achievements.

Performance Feedback and Compensation 6

Introduction

At this point, you've rolled up your sleeves, thrown yourself into your first assignments, and have a few accomplishments under your belt. What happens next? You can expect your manager to respond in some way to the tasks you have completed. Verbal or written feedback can come at almost any point in your work. Your manager may show you a few ways to improve your writing style. A customer may write a memo thanking you for a job well done. Once you have established a pattern of work, or *track record,* your manager's response will be more substantial. If your organization has embraced the new concept of peer evaluation, your teammates will appraise your work. Either way, you will probably receive a *performance appraisal* at the end of six to twelve months on the job. Some kind of compensation for your contributions, such as a raise or more responsibility, may accompany the appraisal. This chapter describes what you can expect, gives you some tips for getting the most out of the feedback you receive, and helps you understand the types of performance compensation that you may receive.

Benefiting from Performance Feedback

To make the most of an appraisal, it is important to understand how an appraisal *helps you,* and to approach it with a positive attitude. All performance feedback, whether positive or negative, offers you an opportunity to learn and do even better in the future. Learning what you did well helps you to repeat that positive contribution. Hearing about areas that need improvement gives you the chance to make corrections. Identifying any areas in which you and your manager set priorities or judged quality differently teaches you the questions to focus on when receiving your next assignment. If you approach the appraisal as an opportunity to learn, with an open, receptive attitude, you can perform a more balanced analysis of the experience and of yourself.

Get Informal Feedback Along the Way

The results of an appraisal should not come as a complete surprise. Ask your manager or teammates for feedback periodically unless they voluntarily provide it. Ask for specific reactions and ways to improve immediately after a significant accomplishment, such as a presentation or a major report. Always be alert for informal feedback, such as comments made during a status meeting. It is less traumatic to get a little negative feedback along the way than to get a lot at the end. You can also correct the problem immediately, which will result in a better formal appraisal when the time comes.

Prepare for the Discussion

If you have advance notice of the formal appraisal, determine the most important challenges you faced during the appraisal period. Evaluate your performance against these challenges. Start by looking at the performance objectives you agreed to with your manager (see Chapter 4), reviewing your log book (see Chapter 3), and writing down how you performed against each goal. Do not concentrate exclusively on the accomplishments. Consider the problems you have had and be prepared to discuss ways to avoid them in the future.

Do not prepare a litany of excuses or blame others for your difficulties; focus the discussion on how *you* performed. This self-review will help you put your past performance in perspective. Surprisingly, when asked to evaluate themselves, most employees do so fairly accurately. An honest self-evaluation prepares you to keep an open mind during the appraisal. The following "Self-Evaluation Worksheet" is an exercise for writing your self-evaluation before your appraisal.

Set Your Attitude

Anticipating a performance review can be a nerve-wracking experience. You may be surprised to hear that the experience can be as stressful for the manager or team as the employee! Even an excellent employee can put a manager on the defensive with a non-receptive attitude. If you are receptive, your manager or teammates are more apt to speak candidly and offer you support. Focus on the appraisal as a chance to learn more about yourself so you can grow to your full potential.

How to Get the Most out of an Appraisal

As with other discussions with your manager or teammates, you will get the most out of the appraisal if you are prepared ahead of time. Here are some pointers to make the most of your appraisal.

Self-Evaluation Worksheet

Complete this worksheet before your company appraisal. Use it as a reference during the appraisal.

How well do you understand your organization's goals and values?

Very little				Very well
1	2	3	4	5

How well do you support your organization's goals and values?

Very little				Very well
1	2	3	4	5

How well do you understand your organization's structure and processes?

Very little				Very well
1	2	3	4	5

How well do you understand your organization's standards and procedures?

Very little				Very well
1	2	3	4	5

How well do you follow your organization's standards and procedures?

Very little				Very well
1	2	3	4	5

How well do you understand your roles and responsibilities and how they fit into the larger work process of your organization?

Very little				Very well
1	2	3	4	5

How well did you communicate and interact with your peers?

Very poorly				Very well
1	2	3	4	5

How well did you communicate and interact with managers?

Very poorly				Very well
1	2	3	4	5

How well did you communicate and interact with your customers?

Very poorly				Very well
1	2	3	4	5

Self-Evaluation Worksheet (continued)

List the skills, tasks, and/or projects you worked on during this appraisal period. For each of them, rate your performance in terms of quality, productivity, and meeting your schedule commitments. Place your ratings in the indicated spaces:

Low quality				High quality
1	2	3	4	5
Low productivity				**High productivity**
1	2	3	4	5
Did not meet any commitments				**Met all commitments**
1	2	3	4	5

Skill/Task/Project	Quality	Productivity	Commitments
______________	______	______	______
	Quality	Productivity	Commitments
______________	______	______	______
	Quality	Productivity	Commitments
______________	______	______	______
	Quality	Productivity	Commitments
______________	______	______	______
	Quality	Productivity	Commitments
______________	______	______	______
	Quality	Productivity	Commitments
______________	______	______	______
	Quality	Productivity	Commitments
______________	______	______	______
	Quality	Productivity	Commitments
______________	______	______	______
	Quality	Productivity	Commitments
______________	______	______	______
	Quality	Productivity	Commitments
______________	______	______	______

Self-Evaluation Worksheet (continued)

Consider your ratings for each skill area, task, and project. Identify why you performed well on some tasks and why you did not on others. From these reflections on your performance, list your strengths and weaknesses below. Identify your development needs. How can they be met?

What are your strengths?

What are your weaknesses?

Develop an action plan of things you can do to maintain and develop your strengths and address your development needs.

Where do you want to go next in your career? In what time frame? What actions need the support of your manager for you to complete your action plan?

1. *Bring your self-evaluation to the discussion.* Because you will probably be at least a little nervous during your appraisal discussion, bring your self-appraisal with you as a reference. Bring along the list of objectives you established with your manager or team. Also bring any indications of how you have performed, such as significant examples of your work or letters of recognition for your achievements. Don't be afraid to refer to these items.

2. *Take notes during the discussion.* It is human nature to focus on and remember the negative. Listen carefully during the appraisal and take notes on *everything* you are told. These notes will be invaluable in putting what your manager said in perspective later.

3. *Ask for specific examples of your performance.* All feedback, whether positive or negative, should include specific examples. Do not be satisfied with generalities such as: "You showed initiative," or "I think you're very innovative." If you do not get specific examples, ask for them directly. Ask specific questions, such as: "In your opinion, when did I show initiative? Are there other areas where I could have been more innovative?"

Specific examples are important because language is very subjective. "Innovative," for example, can mean something different to the manager or teammate than it does to the employee. For example, an employee reads trade journals to stay current and is eager to try the latest software products and techniques. She sees herself as extremely "innovative." Her manager, on the other hand, expects her to find "innovative" ways to improve the work process, such as finding less costly methods to use in her work. Clearly they are talking about two different behaviors.

Without specific examples, each can walk away from the discussion misunderstanding what was said. The manager believes that the need for improving the work process has been communicated. The manager will be assessing this behavior again during the next appraisal period. The employee feels unfairly criticized. She will work even harder to make her knowledge and desire for the latest software known. If the budget for software is small, her manager may keep denying her incessant demands for "innovation." At the next appraisal, there are two negatives to discuss. A downward spiral has begun, caused by miscommunication. You can easily avoid this by asking for specific examples of what your manager means.

4. *If the feedback is positive. . . .*

If the feedback you receive is positive, thank your manager or teammates and feel proud! Many people find it hard to hear good things about themselves and deny the compliment. Resist the urge to say the accomplishment "wasn't a big deal." Be sure to get specific examples of what you did well so you can repeat your performance.

Because it is so difficult for most people to tell others where they need to improve, many managers or teams will limit the appraisal to positives. Probe for any areas where you can improve. Even a great employee can become better.

5. *If the feedback is disappointing. . . .*

Negative feedback is not the end of the world. It is an opportunity to learn and do better in the future. If the feedback you receive is not as glowing as you had hoped, resist the urge to raise your defenses. Do not counter with angry words such as "It was someone else's fault" or "I don't care—this place is unprofessional, anyway." Emotional outbursts will not help. Fully exploring a poor aspect of your performance will cause you some pain; no one is eager to hear exactly how they failed to measure up. You must, however, ask for enough examples so that you fully understand what your manager or teammates mean. This can also help you to determine whether you are dealing with a single incident or a recurring pattern.

Discuss in detail the ways in which you can improve. Ask for examples of good performance you can imitate. Offer your own solution to the problem. Make sure it is one you can live with. If your manager suggests you go back to night school, don't agree unless you can implement the solution. If you can't, suggest an alternative. Be sure your manager agrees that it is an appropriate solution. Ask for a chance to apply the solution immediately if your current assignment does not offer one. You must show your manager or teammates you are willing to address the problem, even if it means investing your own time in correcting it. Set up a follow-up meeting to discuss how well you are applying the solution.

6. *When you and your manager or teammates disagree. . . .*

If you disagree with your evaluation, you may be able to provide additional information your manager or teammates are not aware of. For example, your manager may think you're unapproachable when you are really painfully shy. Most managers are willing to reconsider if you can calmly provide new data. If necessary, ask for another meeting when you can be more objective after considering all the facts.

During the feedback session, be sure to note any areas where you and your manager or teammates differed in rating the importance of an action or an assignment. Did you overestimate the significance of a certain assignment? Finding out what your company values is part of your learning experience. It will help you to set priorities concerning where you spend your time and effort in the future.

After the Appraisal

Review your notes after the appraisal and check them against your self-evaluation. If the appraisal did not go well, you may want to give yourself a day or so to get over any emotional response you are feeling. Later you can be more objective. Is the feedback clear to you after thinking about it for a while? If not, don't hesitate to schedule a follow-up meeting to clarify anything you are unsure of.

Is your manager's or team's opinion valid but something you are unwilling to change? For example, you have been ten minutes late each morning due to the train schedule. Your team is unwilling to accept your staying ten minutes later at night to make up the time. Are you willing to get up an hour earlier to catch the earlier train? Are you willing to accept the consequences of using the later train? Poor or average appraisals often result in lower salary increases in the future. If you are unwilling to change and unwilling to accept the consequences, you may need to look for another job. Does you team's perception of you differ with your own self-perception? Perception equals reality. No matter what you think of yourself, you must deal with the perceptions of others. You see yourself as friendly and upbeat. Your teammates say you have a negative attitude. You must analyze this discrepancy. When joking with your colleagues, do you put down management and complain about the workplace? Consider what others may think of this behavior. In every negative appraisal, there is usually a grain (or more) of truth. Discuss the discrepancy with a trusted coworker whose opinion you respect. Be willing to listen and consider changing your behavior.

If you are having a hard time reconciling a difference between other's perception of your performance and your self-perception, consider the following: Often a strength becomes a weakness if taken to extremes. Because you are proud of your strengths, you may find it hard to recognize any downside to the trait. Before your strengths become weaknesses, identify them. Think about how they can become liabilities if overused. **Exhibit 6.1** is a list of strengths and their counterpart perceived weaknesses when pushed to the extreme or when those strengths are out of balance. Look objectively at your own list of strengths!

Exhibit 6.1. How Strengths Can Become Weaknesses

Strength	(becomes a)	Perceived Weakness
Helpful		Overcommits her time—can't deliver
Attentive to detail		Can't see the big picture
Thorough		Doesn't complete work in a timely manner
Considerate of others		Afraid to take a position—fears alienating others
Assertive		Aggressive, pushy, a "bulldozer"
Not afraid to ask for help		Hasn't learned to do anything by himself
Likes teamwork		Can't work alone
Keeps manager informed		Needs too much of manager's attention
Makes decisions promptly		"Shoots from the hip"

If You Feel You Have Been Wronged

After careful consideration, you may decide you have not been treated fairly. Most companies have a person or department, such as employee relations or human resources, which mediates these kinds of disagreements. Contact them to confidentially discuss your situation before you take any action. They can tell you what the future consequences of a poor appraisal may be and how long the appraisal stays in your file. They may also help you see any grain of truth in the evaluation. Together, you can decide what actions, if any, you should take to remedy the situation. If you work for a company without this kind of resource, find a trusted, experienced coworker who is willing to help you evaluate your situation.

Employees who think they are treated unfairly sometimes write a formal rebuttal to the appraisal. Companies often see rebuttals as a sign of an employee who is disruptive or hostile toward management or the teaming approach. Carefully consider this before you act. You must have facts to back up your rebuttal. This is particularly difficult when the complaint concerns the quality, not timeliness or quantity, or your work. The company may not consider your opinions or testimonials from others relevant.

Fortunately, most appraisal situations don't result in anything worse than the employees feeling a little uncomfortable about areas in which they need to improve. The performance appraisal is one of the many tools available to help you perform to your full potential.

If you don't receive any appraisal by the end of your first year, ask for one. The consequences of not receiving an appraisal range from finding it hard to break a bad habit you've been practicing for a long time to getting laid off without the chance to improve. This may not be fair but it does sometimes happen.

Compensation for Your Contributions

Understanding your company's recognition systems will help you interpret the messages they send. Recognition systems are another form of feedback. They are also a way for you to assess how well you are performing compared to others in the office. What does your company view as significant recognition for employee contributions? Many new employees consider the size of their salary increase to be the most important way the company rewards performance. While raises are important, your company's culture may value getting sent to a special training course over getting a salary increase. Talk to your manager or an experienced, objective coworker about the types of recognition used in your company. Ask for the criteria for receiving them and what limitations, if any, there are on giving them out.

Some of the commonly found forms of performance compensation are:

Types of Compensation

Salary increases

Many companies use a consistent process to determine the raises they give. The company decides what the average salary increase will be for the upcoming 12 months. Managers then rank their employees from highest to lowest performer. Employees at the midpoint of the ranking receive an average raise. Those ranking above the midpoint get a slightly higher percentage; those falling below midpoint receive less than the average or nothing at all.

Salary increases may or may not be given annually depending on a number of factors. Sometimes the size and frequency of raises depend on how well the company is performing. How much you receive and how often you get an increase can fluctuate from year to year.

Occasionally companies adjust the percentages to fit special situations. For instance, an architectural firm may discover that it is paying its interior designers less than those at other local firms. To retain their design talent, the company may give the entire interior design department an above-average raise that year.

You need to understand the specifics of your company's process, including the details of how it is implemented. Without this understanding, many employees become angry over smaller-than-anticipated raises that their manager had no control over.

For example, Joan was accustomed to receiving at least a 10 percent increase in salary each year. This happened during a time of high inflation and a boom in her industry. When inflation dropped and her industry began to slump, the average raise in her company fell to 5 percent. Joan received an above-average salary increase of 7 percent, indicating that she was still performing well. Nevertheless, Joan was furious because 7 percent was lower than her past increases. She complained to her manager who had no power to change the company salary directives. Joan refused to understand and accept the company's policy. She continued to complain to her manager. This eventually became a performance issue in her manager's eyes. The following year, her increase percentage dropped even lower.

How do you find out about the salary planning process in your company? Start with your manager. Your manager should be willing to explain the basics to you. Most managers will not tell you the details of what is planned for you because the plan can change based on your performance appraisal. Your manager will be unable to tell you what salary increases other employees will be receiving. This protects their privacy. When you talk to your manager, don't ask for salary information that cannot reasonably be shared with you.

Other sources of salary planning data include employee relations people and experienced peers. If you decide to talk to another employee, choose someone who is truly knowledgeable and objective. Fellow employees may not fully understand what happens in the salary planning process. If they are not satisfied with their raises, they may inject negative bias into the information they give you.

Bonuses

Bonuses are one-time payments that companies award to employees who bring in more income than others. For example, people in sales often receive a bonus check for a percentage of their sales that year. Bonuses do not raise the employee's regular amount of pay. Not all companies give bonuses. Not all employees in companies that do give bonuses are eligible to receive one.

Awards Many companies have award programs for employees who demonstrate exceptional performance. For example, an employee might win an award for outstanding customer service. Awards can take on a wide variety of forms, such as a cash payment, a dinner or vacation paid for by the company, or a plaque and write-up in the company newsletter. Depending on the award program, nominations for awards can come from management or peer groups. If you win or are even nominated for an award, you can be sure that you have performed well!

Training Being sent to training may be an indication that you are doing well. Your company has a limited amount of money to spend to train its employees. Your manager may decide to invest those training dollars only in the higher performing employees who represent the future of the company. If your manager sends you to a training course, it may very well be an indicator of your good performance. However, if you get sent to a training course that most people in the office also attend, this is not the case. Being sent to a training course in an area you need to improve also does not fall in this category. It does indicate that the company sees you as someone with potential worth cultivating through training.

Special opportunities or assignments Many managers reward employees for good performance by giving them a special opportunity. Special opportunities range from representing the manager at his or her manager's staff meeting to participating on a special task team. Unfortunately, some employees do not realize these opportunities are another form of recognition for their contributions. Rather, they view the assignment as a burden in addition to their normal job. Special assignments are a reward because they offer you an opportunity to learn something new and expand your experience base. They can give you a chance to display your talents to other senior people (this is known as increasing your visibility). Before you complain about an additional assignment you have received, take a minute first to see how you can benefit from the new task.

Increased responsibility

Your manager can increase your responsibility in several ways. Your manager can add more tasks to your job description or have you perform the same tasks on a more critical application, such as for a more demanding customer or on a more complex problem. When increasing your responsibility, your manager is telling you that you have demonstrated the ability to take on tougher challenges. Your manager is expressing faith in your abilities. As with special assignments, some employees do not recognize this as positive feedback. Instead, they complain about the additional workload. Before resisting additional responsibility, assess how you can grow by tackling the new challenge.

Promotion

Promotion to a new job is an obvious type of reward for good performance. A promotion usually includes a change in title and responsibilities and an increase in salary. Sometimes a promotion includes a larger office or an office in a better location, but usually not in first promotions. Do not confuse promotions with a lateral move to a job similar to the one you have been performing. Lateral job changes may indicate that you have not been performing to expectations.

Your promotion may not have an accompanying salary increase. This occurs when there is a limited salary budget or during difficult economic times. New employees find it frustrating when they are promoted with no salary increase. Your manager, however, may see your promotion as an opportunity to groom you by exposure to new departments, functions, and people. Determine if your new responsibilities will give you a broader perspective of the business or greater exposure to higher level management or customers. Ask your manager if a salary increase is planned in the near future. If your manager doesn't tell you directly, ask if your job change is a promotion for good performance or a change because of performance problems.

Assessing Fair Compensation

You may feel that you are being under-compensated for your performance. Perhaps you think that your coworkers have more responsibility than you do. Maybe you believe you should have received a bigger raise. You may feel that your manager or teammates have overlooked some important aspect of your contribution. You are beginning to think you are a victim of discrimination. In most cases, when employees feel under-compensated, they have overvalued their contribution to the company by failing to compare it to the contributions of others. Before you take any action on your feelings, assess the situation using the following steps:

1. *Understand the rules.* Make sure you fully understand the criteria for receiving the type of additional compensation you are seeking. Find out if there were limitations on giving the compensation. For example, if you think it was unfair that you didn't get a bonus, make sure that your company gave bonuses that year. Maybe no one received one!

2. *Evaluate your performance.* Using the "Self-Evaluation Worksheet" on pages 87–89 of this chapter, perform a self-assessment of your performance. Using the criteria for the type of compensation you are seeking, identify your accomplishments that meet the criteria. Try to be honest about which accomplishments are truly significant and which are incidental.

3. *Compare your accomplishments.* Evaluate how your performance rates when compared to the contributions of your peers. This is not easy. When you are busy with your own tasks, it is difficult if not impossible to know all facets of your coworkers' performances. Focus on comparing the quantity, quality, and significance of your major achievements with that of your peers.

4. *Get additional input from someone else.* It is hard to admit your shortcomings. It helps to get additional feedback from someone who has observed your work. Don't take comfort in the condolences of friends and family members. They have only heard your side of the story. Since giving and receiving honest feedback can be touchy, ask for input from a senior person who is experienced in coaching less-seasoned employees. This feedback is likely to be more objective. You are also less likely to ruin a good relationship with a peer!

How to Ask for a Raise

After you have completed the steps above, you may decide that you are truly under-compensated. You must carefully plan and conduct a discussion on this subject. Do not burst into your manager's office with a statement like "I'm not living the lifestyle I want to live so I need a bonus" or "Please give me a raise because my wife is about to have a baby." This approach will probably not win you any additional compensation. You are more likely to be successful if you do the following (which will also work if your company allows self-directed work teams to decide salaries and compensation):

1. *Schedule a meeting ahead of time with your manager.* Your manager will perform better in this situation if you allow time for preparation. Give advanced notice so your manager can collect pertinent data, including information about your performance. Advanced notice will focus your manager's attention on the topic at hand. Do not spring this conversation on a manager who is distracted with other concerns.

2. *Keep the discussion focused on your performance.* Do not use the argument that others make more than you do. You have no influence over anyone else's compensation. In addition, the salary of others is none of your business. Revealing that you know what peers are making will not bolster your case. Instead, use the analysis you did in your "Self-Evaluation Worksheet." Focus the conversation on what you accomplished and how it meets the criteria for the compensation you are seeking.

3. *Stay factual, avoid emotion.* Keep the conversation focused on your analysis, not on how you feel about the situation. Resist accusing your manager of being unfair. Your accusations may make your manager feel defensive and less open-minded about your request.

4. *Take notes.* Take notes to help you put the conversation into perspective later.

5. *Practice the conversation.* Ask a friend or family member to pretend to be your manager. Practice the conversation. Have them respond in a variety of ways so you can determine how you will react. If you don't have someone to practice with, rehearse the discussion in your mind.

6. *Prepare for the outcome.* If you succeed with your request, congratulations! Many employees do. Be sure to thank your manager. If you are not successful, you need to understand why. If the manager does not offer an explanation, probe for one. You may learn

that there is a restriction on your manager's ability to give you the compensation. In this case, you need to do more homework on how things happen in your office. (Read Chapter 3.) Your manager may not agree that you deserve additional compensation. In this case, the discussion is apt to turn into an appraisal discussion. Turn to the pointers in the beginning of this chapter for how to handle this type of meeting.

Summary

If you practice the skills described in this section—performance skills—you will improve the quality of your work. The next section describes another dimension of your performance—interpersonal skills. How well you work with the people you see daily is a significant factor in how successful you are and how you are perceived.

INTERPERSONAL SKILLS

Section III

Communicating Effectively

7

Introduction

You may not realize it but you spend a major portion of your day at work communicating in any one of many forms. Whether you are coordinating with a coworker to produce a report, phoning a supplier, or participating in a staff meeting, you are using your communications skills. Since communicating is such an integral part of work, it is extremely important to learn the basics of both written and verbal communications.

Effective communication is a complex subject. You can spend your entire career perfecting these skills. There are quite a few books on the market devoted to the many aspects of writing and speaking. This chapter will show you some basic concepts of communication and give you specific pointers on a number of communication forms you may be using on the job.

Power of the Pen—Written Communication

Written communications are less complex than verbal communications. Written communications are one-way, meaning the person sending the written message does not receive immediate feedback or response from the message recipient. Written communications may be more difficult because you cannot adjust what you are trying to say based on the immediate feedback of the recipient. Written communications are also more permanent than other communications. The record of what you write remains for others to refer to over time.

The success of your written communication depends on three factors. Consider how well you have addressed each factor when communicating in writing in the workplace.

Factor 1: The Message

The most obvious factor in written communication is the message itself. The message is **what** is being conveyed. The success of the message depends on its clarity. How well have you stated your purpose for communicating? Is your intent to:

- Inform? ("The shipment was sent on November 22 by Federal Express. . . .")
- Request? ("Please send me a price list and specification for your product. . . .")
- Persuade? ("Please consider the low cost and high quality of our product. . . .")

Clearly stating your reason for writing in the opening paragraph helps the reader prepare to understand the rest of the message. It also lets the person know what action, if any, is required in response.

A second aspect of message clarity is the completeness of the information. All relevant data must be conveyed for the message to be effective. For example, if you are requesting a quote from a supplier, be sure to include the part number, the number of parts you are interested in buying, and the date when you need to receive the quote. Of course, you would clearly include in the letterhead the address for the reply. The receiver can then supply exactly the information you requested when you need it.

Factor 2: How the Message Is Sent

You have several choices about how you will deliver your message. One choice you will make is the medium for communicating. In some environments, an electronic message could imply urgency while a paper document could signify more time for a reply. A handwritten memo could indicate that the message is still in draft form; a typed message could denote formality.

Another decision that will influence your message is the style and tone of the language you use. First person (using "I" or "we") sounds more personal and immediate than third person ("The ABC Company"). Similarly, industry jargon, acronyms, and colloquial phrases add an element of informality. Finally, the shades of meaning of the specific words you select communicate to the reader your position on your topic. Consider the following sentences:

1. I can accommodate your recommendation.
2. I can agree with your recommendation.
3. I can support your recommendation.

Clearly, the sentences convey the increasing strength of the writer's accord with the recommendation. Be aware of the effects your choice of words has on the reader. Be sure you truly wish to use the shade of meaning you have selected. As part of your ongoing orientation to your office environment, familiarize yourself with how your office implements each of these aspects of written communications. You will probably see different techniques used for communicating within your department or unit, between other units within the company, and outside the company.

Factor 3: The Reader

The final critical factor in the success of written communication is the state of the reader. There are two elements to consider. First you must think about the reader's ability to understand the message. Does the reader understand the:

- Words? Your reader could come from a different country and not have full command of the English language.
- Colloquialisms or jargon? Your reader could come from a different part of this country or a different company or industry where people use a different set of colloquialisms or jargon.

- Anologies and examples? Your reader might not be an avid baseball fan as you are and misunderstand your reference.
- Topic? Your reader might not have your background or experience.
- Circumstances? Your reader might not be aware of the events motivating you to send your message.

You must also think about your reader's attitude toward the subject you are writing about. Is the topic one that makes your reader angry every time it is brought up, regardless of how well it is written? If so, you might want to keep your message concise and to the point so that the reader can quickly grasp the message and be done with it. If the subject is a favorite one of the reader, you can probably afford to expand a little on the message with interesting relevant information.

Different Types of Business Writing

Anytime you send a written message in the office, no matter how formal or what medium you choose, the three critical factors just described must be considered when you write it. Here are some additional pointers and potential pitfalls to avoid for some of the specific types of writing you will be doing.

Notes and Messages

Notes and messages are short, informal types of written communication used to provide brief bits of information to the receiver. Notes and messages may be written on a scrap of paper or quickly sent via electronic mail (E-mail). A note or message might look like this:

> Sue,
>
> Ed called at 1:37 with questions about the budget. He'd like you to call him back at x9090.
>
> Bob x5678

Pointers

1. **Write legibly**. Nothing is more frustrating than deciphering illegible handwriting.

2. **Include your name and phone extension**. Even close associates might not recognize your handwriting. Save them the time of looking up the number.

3. **Leave notes where they can be easily seen**. This may be on a clean desk area, stuck to a door or computer terminal. If the note is at all personal, such as a phone message from the person's spouse, leave the message in a more discreet place such as the person's chair, where casual passersby will not accidentally read the contents.

4. **Use notes to convey ordinary, day-to-day types of information**. Do not drop a note on your manager's desk informing him or her that a critical shipment that affects an important contract will be delivered two weeks late. The importance of the message dictates the way it should be conveyed.

5. **Never write anything you don't want others to see**. You never know who else might read your note. A note containing your candid opinion of how poorly a meeting you attended went could be accidentally dropped on the floor or stuck in with other papers. Similarly, electronic mail messages can be forwarded to someone else or printed in hard copy and read by someone other than your intended recipient. Do not assume that the recipient will protect your confidentiality. Private messages printed on public printers are often read by others. When you leave a note, consider how it will reflect on you if ANYONE reads it.

6. **Don't leave a note when your message should be delivered in person**. Bad news and personal emergencies are best conveyed quickly and face-to-face.

7. **Don't leave a note that requires a timely response and think that you have done your job**. Will the person see it in time to respond? If there is any possibility that the recipient will not see the message in time, check back at some later time (but before the deadline is near) to see that the message was received. If not, you may need to personally find the target of your message or ask a secretary for help.

Memos and letters

Memoranda (memos for short) and letters are more formal means of communicating than notes. They are used when a significant amount of data needs to be conveyed; when the situation requires formality, such as communicating to a superior or customer, or the information needs to be referenced or saved for use at a later time. Many offices still distribute their memos and letters in hard copy (printed on paper). As offices automate, E-mail is being used instead since the distribution is easier and faster.

There are five worksheets following these pointers for memos and letters. They will take you through the entire process for writing effective business memos. Use the worksheets until the writing process becomes second nature to you. The worksheets are: "Message Summary," "The Reader," "Data Organization," "Text," and "Review."

Pointers

1. **Select a subject line (title) that concisely conveys the contents of the memo**. This will help a busy reader who has to prioritize his or her mail. It also helps find the memo if it needs to be referenced later.

2. **Understand the audience for your memo before you begin**. What level of knowledge do they have about the subject or the circumstances of the memo topic? How much attention to detail will the reader be able to pay to what you write? Adjust the contents to the reader's level. You do not want to leave your reader mystified, bored, or impatient with your writing.

3. **Find out what review and approval is required before you distribute your memo**. Many managers do not allow any communication to be sent before they look at it. A manager may want to review memos to maintain a consistent office style, to determine the thoroughness of the message, to check your understanding of the level of the reader, or even ensure that the contents are legal. If no approvals are necessary, have a more experienced person review your first few memos to ensure you meet office standards.

4. **Include a distribution list**. This is a courtesy if your memo is going to more than one person, so all recipients know who else received a copy.

5. **Remember, you do not know if your memo will be read by others who are not on your distribution list.** Keep this in mind if your memo conveys negative opinions, personal information, or company-sensitive material. Many companies have special procedures or envelopes for use in these circumstances.

6. **Mark DRAFT across the top of each page of your working copies.** Prematurely read drafts, which may be full of spelling errors and incomplete sentences, will then not appear to be your final submittal.

7. **Proofread everything you write before you distribute it.** Typos, misspellings, and incorrect grammar detract from the message you are sending and leave the reader with the impression that you are careless or have poor writing skills. Use electronic spelling checkers, dictionaries, or a good secretary to minimize these errors.

Memo-Writing Worksheet 1: Message Summary

What is your message? This is a fairly obvious yet frequently ignored first thing to do! Why is this the important first step? It clarifies your desired result and establishes a framework for the remaining steps. In **one** sentence, write down the purpose of your memo.

The purpose of this memo is to:

____

____

____

Memo-Writing Worksheet 2: The Reader

Success in communicating to your readers equates to the success of your memo. Therefore, you want to identify your readers so you speak their language at their level of understanding.

Who will receive copies of this memo?

Direct Distribution: ______________________________

____

"Carbon Copy": ______________________________

____

Potential Forwarding: ______________________________

____

How much does the prime reader know about my topic or need to be reminded about?

____

____

Does the prime reader know the key facts behind my subject?

Fact 1: ____________ ____ YES ____ NO

Fact 2: ____________ ____ YES ____ NO

Fact 3: ____________ ____ YES ____ NO

Fact 4: ____________ ____ YES ____ NO

Fact 5: ____________ ____ YES ____ NO

What are the primary concerns of my prime reader? (e.g., financial results, project schedule)

____

____

What is my reader's sphere of influence?

____

____

What "language" does my reader speak, e.g., finance, marketing, sales?

____

____

Memo-Writing Worksheet 3: Data Organization

The way you organize your memo depends on the message you are conveying, although the basic outline below works for most. To develop your memo, start with a simple outline. Add to each level of the outline with increasing detail until the memo is complete. This technique ensures the message flows in a logical manner. It also helps highlight which points are key and which are less important.

I. **Introduction**

  A. Purpose of memo

  B.

II. **Background Information** (if necessary)

  A.

  B.

  C.

III. **Main Message** (may be organized chronologically, or in a list by priority, logical sequence, or other scheme that clarifies the message.)

  A.

  B.

  C.

IV. **Conclusions** (e.g., request for reader action, summary of informative memo, next steps)

  A.

  B.

  C.

V. **Signoff** (how to reach you, thanks for assistance, invite readers to contact you with any questions and concerns)

  A.

  B.

Memo-Writing Worksheet 4: Text

Now that you have your detailed outline complete, your information needs to be converted to text. Having completed Worksheet 3, this will be an easy task. Just turn each outline section into a paragraph of your memo.

Remember:

- ***Keep your language simple.***
  Avoid pretentious words and complex sentences. This focuses the reader's attention and stresses your point.
- ***Make your subject line or title meaningful.***
- ***Always include the date of the memo.***

Finally, you need to add the finishing touches. Check with a secretary to find out the format used for memos in your office. You will probably need to know how to include:

_____ Date

_____ Memo distribution list—for both direct and "carbon copy" recipients

_____ Subject or title line

_____ Your address and phone number

_____ Memo priority—if relevant

_____ Your salutation and name

Now write your draft memo.

Memo-Writing Worksheet 5: Review

Once you have completed the memo, put yourself in your reader's shoes and step through the memo again. Here is a checklist for ensuring that you have a winning memo.

Does the memo . . .

Spell all recipients' names correctly?	_____YES	_____NO
Have no misspelled words or incorrect punctuation?	_____YES	_____NO
Progress logically?	_____YES	_____NO
Follow a smooth transition from paragraph to paragraph?	_____YES	_____NO
Avoid little-known acronyms?	_____YES	_____NO
Define new terms and concepts each time they are introduced?	_____YES	_____NO
Stress the right points?	_____YES	_____NO
Communicate the right message?	_____YES	_____NO

Documents

Documents are the most formal type of written communication. They are usually created for "official" reasons, such as to capture contractual agreements, document procedures, convey contractually required data to a customer, or respond to an auditor's request. Like memos and letters, documents are often transmitted by hard copy, although electronic transmittal is beginning to be more common.

Pointers

1. **Look into the existence of an office document template**. Adhere to it strictly if you find one. You will probably find a guideline that describes the required or preferred style and format for the documents you must produce. Although you might have a more concise or logical way to format your information, the official format may be required by the customer or for legal reasons.

2. **Find out if a review and approval cycle is required**. This is likely, since a document is usually formal or official. In addition to your immediate manager, higher-level managers, your legal department, and others may have to become involved. Be sure to learn if the additional parties approving the document for release are required to do so in a particular order. For example, the president of the company may not want to sign, indicating approval, until the legal department has completed its review.

3. **Leave enough time to complete a review process if one is required**. Many employees fail to do this, which puts due dates in jeopardy. Remember that others in the cycle are busy people, too, and need time to read and sign the document. Remember also that reviewers might request changes to the document before they will sign it. Sometimes a change can cause the entire review process to start over again! Plan enough time for some changes to be made. Find out from others in your unit how long a review cycle typically takes.

The Spoken Word—Verbal Communications

Verbal communication skills are slightly more complex than written communication skills. In verbal communications, you receive and must interpret immediate feedback, both verbal and nonverbal. You will not always have time to compose what you want to say in advance. The audience does not always have the opportunity to prepare to receive and understand the message. The three success factors for written skills apply to verbal skills as well, with an additional factor to consider—changing roles.

Factor 1: The Message

When you speak, your message must be clear and complete. This factor is critical when you are speaking to a person who has only a little time to talk with you. You must get your points across quickly and succinctly. If you are unable to do this, it might be better for you to postpone the conversation to a time when your audience can pay more attention to you.

Factor 2: How the Message Is Sent

As in writing, when verbally sending a message you also have choices about how your message is conveyed. If the message is informal, you may choose to tell your audience when you run into them casually, at the coffee area or when they pass by your desk. Alternatively, a more formal message may require you to set up an appointment or meeting.

Also like written communications, you must decide how your message will be influenced by the style you use. Since verbal communications usually occur face-to-face, your message delivery now includes your tone of voice and body language. Facial expressions, eye contact, your posture, and the volume and pitch of your voice—all can influence your listener.

Factor 3: The Listener

The state of your listener is equally important in speaking as it is in writing. When you are face-to-face, you have an opportunity to assess the degree to which the listener is receiving your message by watching body language and listening to responses. Pay attention to these response cues! There are three elements to consider.

The **first two elements** are similar to the writing skills factors. You must judge the listener's ability to understand the message. If the listener is not a native English speaker, you may have to slow down your delivery rate. If the listener is partially deaf, you may have to speak more distinctly. You must also think about the listener's attitude towards your subject. You will probably be able to tell from the look on the listener's face whether he or she is bored, getting angry, or finds the topic fascinating.

The new **third element** is the listener's ability to pay attention to your conversation. If your audience is tired, distracted, under a lot of stress or not feeling well, they may not be taking in a good part of what you are saying. If your message is important, it is usually best to try to reschedule your conversation for a later time.

Factor 4: Changing Roles

Most verbal communications are two-way. Two or more people participate in a conversation. That means that you will play the role of both the message deliverer *and* the message receiver (or listener). To be an effective verbal communicator, it is important that you also develop good listening skills.

An effective listener tries to actively understand what is being said. Repeat what you heard in your own terms to ensure that you understood. Ask questions if you need clarification. Refrain from attacking or judging the person delivering the message. Focusing on the content of what is said opens up the channels of communication so you can better tune-in to the person you are communicating with.

Different Types of Verbal Communications

The four factors just described are important whenever you communicate verbally. Following are some typical ways we communicate verbally, with additional pointers and potential pitfalls to avoid when you are a speaker and when you change roles to that of a listener.

Conversations

Conversations are dialogues between two or more people which can occur in both formal and informal settings. Informal conversations, in which your words and body language are casual, are held with friends, your coworkers, or those people who invite you to be informal (for example, a manager who wants a less hierarchical relationship with his or her employees). The topic of informal conversations can range from work to personal affairs. Formal conversations, where you communicate with the utmost professionalism, are conducted with *power* people, such as managers and customers. Generally, formal conversations are limited to work subjects.

Pointers as a message sender:

1. **Modulate your voice appropriately when talking to people**. Avoid yelling, speaking too softly, or whining.

2. **Maintain eye contact with your audience**. This will enhance your effectiveness as a communicator. People who avoid eye contact may appear distracted, overly nervous, or evasive.

3. **Be sensitive to how busy the other person is and whether you have let a conversation continue too long**. Signs that you should bring the conversation to an end are:

- Your listener begins shuffling or reading papers on the desk.
- Your listener provides abrupt responses to your questions.
- Your listener begins edging away from you.

4. **Be sensitive to what is important to the listener**. This is especially true in formal conversations. Is it important for the manager or customer to receive a lot of detail or just a summary of your issue? Given the listener's responsibilities, which aspects of your topic are important?

5. **Keep the discussion focused on the areas that are in the listener's realm of influence in formal conversations concerning a problem**. Talking to a manufacturing manager about problems in marketing might not be an effective use of the manufacturing manager's time.

6. **Have an agenda**. For your formal conversations this is necessary so you can make all your points succinctly and logically.

7. **A subject that is not controversial or offensive to you may be to someone else**. Upsetting someone in a casual conversation can jeopardize your ability to work with that person later. Areas of potential danger include topics related to religion, politics, and sex.

8. **Confidential and personal conversations you do not want shared are often at risk of being over-**

heard. Remember: rest rooms, partitioned offices, and hallways are not private places.

9. **Once you tell someone something, you no longer control who else might receive your words**. Gossip, judgmental statements, and sarcastic or angry remarks can be repeated or your comments misquoted out of context.

10. **Poor grammar, overuse of slang, lack of eye contact, and sloppy physical appearance are parts of your communication**. These can all leave negative impressions with your audience.

11. **Don't assume you can be informal with management or customers in your attempt to establish rapport with them**. New employees should take the lead from the senior person in determining the level of formality of the conversation.

Pointers as a listener:

1. **Show the same courtesy to people speaking to you as you expect from them**. Don't start reading or working on your computer when someone is trying to talk to you. If you are very busy or trying to meet a deadline, politely say so and reschedule the conversation for a later time.

2. **Use body language to communicate interest and understanding in what you are hearing**. Eye contact, facial expressions, and head nods indicate you are listening.

3. **Avoid reacting to what you hear before the message is completely delivered**. An emotional or angry reaction may be premature and hinder effective communication.

4. **Don't assume you understand what you have heard without getting clarification**. Everyone enters a conversation with preconceived ideas derived from their unique set of experiences. Two techniques for ensuring un-

derstanding are paraphrasing and elaboration of the speaker's comments. Sometimes misunderstandings, which could have been avoided through these clarification techniques, prevent coworkers from working effectively together.

5. **Know the difference between something that is told to you in confidence and what is for public knowledge**. If you are unsure, ask. Repeating someone's personal news or unreleased information to the office can gain you the reputation of being a gossip and untrustworthy.

Telephone

Verbal communications via the telephone are a special case of the conversation. When using the telephone, the communication remains two-way (unless, of course, you are talking to an answering machine). Since it is not face-to-face, however, an additional set of pointers apply.

Pointers as a sender:

1. **Identify yourself immediately when you initiate a phone call**. Assuming that your voice will be recognized and launching into a discussion can put the person on the other end of the line in an embarrassing position if he or she, in fact, does not recognize who is calling.

2. **Have all materials you need to reference near the phone before you make your call**. You will be wasting the listener's time if you have to keep putting the phone down to go get something.

3. **Since you cannot see the other person, be especially sensitive to interrupting them**. Ask if this is a good time to talk or whether you should call back. If you should call back, arrange a specific time so the interruption is not repeated.

4. **You cannot always tell if you have reached someone who is using a speaker phone**. Be aware that someone else could be listening to your call. If you need to use a speaker phone, be sure to tell the other person that others are hearing the conversation.

5. **Remember that your listener hears your voice tone without seeing your body language**. Your voice could reflect that you are upset about a situation completely unrelated to the phone call, yet the listener could perceive that the emotion is directed at her.

6. **Mobile phones, both at home and in the car, are easily intercepted**. Be careful not to discuss company proprietary information on a mobile phone.

7. **Don't eat while you are conducting a telephone conversation**.

8. **Don't make your telephone conversations any longer than you need to be**. Some signs that your listener is ready to get off include short answers to questions, the sound of the listener typing in the background, and hints about wrapping up.

Pointers as a listener:

1. **Find out if there is a common greeting when answering the phone at your company**. Some companies prefer that you answer by stating the company's name and your department, while others want people to supply their name and position. Remember that you are representing your company whenever you answer the phone in the office.

2. **Take complete and accurate messages when picking up calls for someone else who is not available**. Getting the caller's name, phone number, time of call, and reason for calling will help your coworkers to be more effective.

3. **Don't be tempted to keep working on whatever you were doing when the phone rang since the person on the other end of the line cannot see you**. You can be betrayed by the noise on your keyboard clacking away or when you fail to respond to a question. Focus your attention on the call to make it more effective.

4. **Don't allow yourself to be held hostage by a phone caller**. Keep your responses on the business being dis-

cussed. If you are busy but interested in the information, arrange for the caller to call at a more convenient time.

5. **Sometimes you should allow disruptive calls to roll over to a secretary or an answering machine if your responsibilities do not require immediate phone response**. In particular, if you are holding a meeting in your office, try to arrange for phone coverage so you can focus on the meeting. If this cannot be arranged, keep the calls as brief as possible out of respect for those in the meeting.

Meetings

Meetings are also a special case of communication. In this situation, more than two people get together to exchange opinions and make decisions. Since you can play the role of the person running the meeting (the facilitator) or that of a participant, two sets of pointers are provided.

Pointers as the meeting facilitator:

1. **Establish an agenda before the meeting**. Try to distribute the agenda before the meeting so all the participants are familiar with the topics to be discussed and can prepare ahead of time. Assign each topic a time duration for discussion. Order agenda items based on their importance. Use the time estimate and order as a guide for keeping the meeting on track.

2. **Distribute all materials to be discussed or referenced at the meeting to the participants ahead of time**. This helps everyone come to the meeting prepared and avoids time wasted if the participants have to read the materials at the meeting.

3. **Also distribute ahead of time the list of attendees at the meeting**. This is a further indication of the type of meeting that is planned and allows people to coordinate items ahead of time, if needed.

4. **Ensure a conference room is available and reserved BEFORE you notify people of the meeting**. It is inconvenient and embarrassing to have to reschedule your meeting due to conference room unavailability.

5. **Send background information to the less knowledgeable people ahead of time so they can contribute**. Sometimes your meeting audience will have a range of knowledge of your topics. Time can be wasted and attention lost while bringing part of the group up to speed.

6. **Try to start the meeting on time so you don't waste participants' time**. Arrive ahead of time to ensure that the chairs are set up as you'd like and that any needed equipment and material (overhead projector, flip charts, markers, etc.) are in the meeting room and working.

7. **Be flexible, but try to keep the meeting discussion focused on your agenda topics**. Sometimes straying off the agenda is helpful when the new information contributes to the purpose of the meeting. If, however, you do not understand the connection, ask for an explanation. Tangents that interest only a few meeting attendees are topics for other meetings, not yours. As the facilitator, you can ask that the topic be addressed *off-line*, meaning outside of your meeting.

Pointers as a meeting participant:

1. **Let the meeting facilitator know as far in advance as possible if you will be late or cannot attend a meeting**. Don't just fail to show up! The meeting may be counting on you for a particular piece of information. If you can't attend, find out if you can send an alternate.

2. **Be on time for all meetings**. It wastes others' time if they have to go over information a second time because you weren't there to hear it the first time.

3. **Come prepared to participate at any meeting to which you are invited**. If materials are distributed ahead of time, read them before the meeting. If you were assigned to complete specific tasks before the meeting, have them completed. Being prepared minimizes wasted time, as well as avoids having to schedule a second (unnecessary) meeting.

4. **Keep your focus on the meeting at hand and its purpose**. Sure, there are times when your attention will

wander—that's normal. However, initiating conversations on tangent topics or having a side discussion with the person next to you also wastes time and may make you an unwelcome attendee at future meetings.

5. **Avoid personal attacks or putting people on the spot**. This can happen when you perceive that other participants do not share your views or are not as knowledgeable as you are. Although you may see some people do this, it does not help you build a good working relationship with others. Such attacks reduce your coworkers' ability to trust you. Contribute your alternate views constructively or have the conversation outside the meeting with the person with whom you disagree.

Presentations/Briefings

Presentations and briefings are a hybrid of verbal and written communications. Perhaps that is why they are so difficult! Usually written slides are prepared in advance, which are presented with an oral briefing. If you are a listener, your behavior can influence the success or failure of the presentation. If you are the presenter, pay equal attention to both the written and spoken facets of your briefing.

We provide pointers for both situations, followed by five worksheets to guide you through writing an effective presentation. Those worksheets are "Message Summary," "The Audience," "Data Organization," "Charts," and "Review." Use these worksheets for your presentations and briefing until the process becomes natural to you.

Pointers as a presenter

1. **Find out how to operate any needed audiovisual equipment ahead of time**. Come early to the presentation and learn how to turn on/off microphones, overhead projectors, VCRs, etc. This also will ensure that the equipment works.

2. **Know in advance who will attend your presentation**. Be sure you know by name and face any key people relevant to your topic.

3. **Speak slowly and distinctly when you give your presentation**. If you are nervous, you will probably rush. Consciously slow down.

4. **Don't read your charts**. Your audience can do that without you. Use your charts only as a road map for your presentation.

5. **"Grease the skids" on controversial topics**. If you think your presentation could provoke an adverse or hostile reaction from some of your listeners, talk to them before the briefing to try to work out differences or, at least, to get their cooperation in not disrupting your briefing.

6. **Limit each presentation chart to a single point**. Some people like to read ahead during the presentation, either looking at points on the charts which have not yet been addressed or, if they have a paper copy of the briefing, looking at later charts. The problem that can result is the person reacts to points you have not yet clarified and breaks the flow of your presentation. In addition to limiting each chart to one point, consider whether or not you have to provide handouts of your presentation before you give it.

Pointers as a listener

1. **Don't arrive late to a presentation**. It is rude and can be disruptive to walk in midway through a briefing. If you absolutely cannot avoid coming in late, slip in quietly and take the closest seat to the door you can find.

2. **Don't leave in the middle of a speech**. This, too, is rude and can be disruptive. If you must leave and know in advance, choose a seat close to the door so you can slip out with minimal distraction.

3. **Remember that you are providing the speaker nonverbal feedback with your body language**. He or she can see if you are writing, yawning, sleeping, or listening attentively.

4. **Don't carry on conversations with your neighbors**. Side conversations are distracting to others who are trying to listen. If you have a question about the presentation, share it with everyone. Chances are that someone else in the audience has a similar question.

Presentation/Briefing Worksheet 1: Message Summary

What is your message? This is a fairly obvious yet frequently ignored first thing to do! Why is this the important first step? It clarifies your desired result and establishes a framework for the remaining steps. In **one** sentence, write down the purpose of your presentation.

The purpose of this presentation is to:

____

____

____

____

____

____

____

____

Presentation/Briefing Worksheet 2: The Audience

Success in communicating to your listeners equates to the success of your presentation. Therefore, you want to identify your audience so you talk their language at their level of understanding.

How much does the audience know about my topic? ____

____

Does the audience know the key facts behind by presentation?

Fact 1: ______________________________ ____ YES ____ NO

Fact 2: ______________________________ ____ YES ____ NO

Fact 3: ______________________________ ____ YES ____ NO

Fact 4: ______________________________ ____ YES ____ NO

Fact 5: ______________________________ ____ YES ____ NO

What are the primary concerns of my audience? (example: to get an overall understanding of the topic? to make a decision based on your analysis? to approve your recommendations?)

____

____

____

____

What is my audience's sphere of influence?

____

____

____

____

What "language" does my audience speak, e.g., finance, marketing, sales?

____

____

____

____

Presentation/Briefing Worksheet 3: Data Organization

The way you organize your presentation depends on the message you are conveying, although the basic outline below works for most. To develop your presentation, start with a simple outline. Add to each level of the outline with increasing detail until the briefing is complete. This technique ensures the message flows in a logical manner. It also helps highlight which points are key and which are less important.

I. **Introduction or agenda** (gets you on the stage)

A.

B.

II. **Background** (establishes common ground with the audience)

A.

B.

C.

III. **Main Message** (the core of the presentation)

A.

B.

C.

IV. **Conclusions** (gains audience buy-in)

A.

B.

C.

V. **Summary** (gets you off the stage)

A.

B.

Sample Outline for a Status Briefing

- ***I. Agenda***
- ***II. Background***
  - *A. Objectives*
  - *B. Assumptions*
  - *C. Approach*
- ***III. Main Message***
  - *A. Progress/accomplishments*
  - *B. Schedules*
  - *C. Issues/concerns/problems*
- ***IV. Conclusions***
  - *A. Conclusion summary*
  - *B. Recommendations*
- ***V. Summary—next steps***

Sample Outline for a Persuasive Briefing

- ***I. Agenda***
- ***II. Background***
  - *A. Objective*
  - *B. Problem statement*
  - *C. Why important*
    - *1. Historical data*
    - *2. Impacts*
- ***III. Main Message***
  - *A. Options—description*
  - *B. Comparative analysis*
  - *C. Recommendations*
- ***IV. Conclusions***
  - *A. Summarized selected recommendation*
  - *B. Summarized benefits*
- ***V. Summary—next steps***

Presentation/Briefing Worksheet 4: Charts

Now that you have your detailed outline complete, your information needs to be converted to charts. If you completed Worksheet 3, this will be an easy task. Just follow these steps:

1. Draw a box around each major topic area (usually one box per each Roman numeral section of your outline). This is the first pass at creating your charts.

2. Examine each "chart" (box) and determine if there are too many words on the chart for the message to be conveyed quickly and easily to your audience. If so, divide your chart into two new boxes, according to the next level of detail in your outline.

3. Repeat step 2 for each chart until you are satisfied that each chart is clear and concise.

4. Replace each outline number with a bullet, dash, or other character used by your organization.

Remember:

- ***Limit one major topic to a page.***
  - This focuses the audience's attention and stresses your point.
  - This prevents your audience from getting ahead of you in the briefing.

- ***Keep bullets to one line (don't wrap)***
  - This helps your points to stand out.
  - This helps you not to read your charts when presenting them.

- ***Use graphics (diagrams, matrices, flow charts, etc.)***
  - Pictures can convey your message more concisely than text.
  - Avoid complicated "eye charts," e.g., unreadable diagrams or overly complex pictures.

Presentation/Briefing Worksheet 5: Review

Once you have completed the presentation, put yourself in your audience's shoes and step through the presentation again. Here is a checklist for ensuring that you have a winning presentation.

Does the presentation . . .

Progress logically?	_____YES	_____NO
Transition well from chart to chart?	_____YES	_____NO
Avoid little-known acronyms?	_____YES	_____NO
Define new terms and concepts each time they are introduced?	_____YES	_____NO
Stress the right points?	_____YES	_____NO
Communicate the right message?	_____YES	_____NO

Summary

This chapter has covered just a few of the many ways you may find yourself communicating in the workplace. Never stop striving to improve your communications skills. The level of your abilities will make a decided impression on those receiving your message.

Strong communications skills, coupled with the pointers in the next chapter, "Managing Office Relationships," will help you interact as effectively as possible with the people you deal with on your job.

Managing Office Relationships

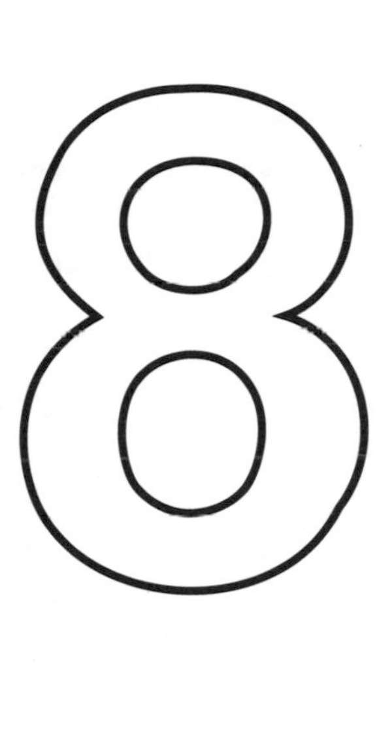

Introduction

There is hardly a job in this country that does not require interaction with others as a regular part of the position. Almost all of us work with supervisors, coworkers, service providers, or customers. Managing these office relationships effectively is a vital aspect of the job. This chapter identifies some of the key relationships you will have to establish and maintain, and provides tips for doing so successfully. Every office relationship consists of the behavior of only two people: *you* and someone else. For any office relationship, you will be successful if you keep in mind the following two maxims.

1. *Understand the other person—then have patience and respect for that person.*

We all come to the workplace with our own unique set of knowledge and experiences which, in turn, define our values. No two people are alike in this regard, although you will find people who are more similar to you than others are. These similar people are the ones we tend to get along with easily. When you encounter a difference of opinion, try to get to the root of why the person thinks the way he or she does. After probing for a reason, you may be surprised to find your mind has been changed. If not, try to value the differences, knowing that when it comes to your work, the differences of experiences and opinions will result in more creative and thoroughly-considered solutions to work problems.

2. *Understand how your opinions and behavior affect those around you.*

You can't control other people's behavior, but you can certainly control your own. You need to be sensitive to the fact that because people are different, they won't necessarily respond to your behaviors and opinions as you expect they will. At a minimum, you need to exhibit courtesy, good manners, and an understanding of your group's norms so you don't violate them. If you haven't read Chapters 2 and 3, now is a good time to review ways you can make a positive impression on people and learn about your organization's norms.

Supervisor Relationships

One of the most important relationships you will manage will be with your supervisor. Many employees, old and new, seem to have misconceptions about their supervisor's abilities and responsibilities. These misconceptions get in the way of being able to get along with the person. Eight of those misconceptions are included here.

Eight Myths About Supervisors

1. All supervisors are out to get you—therefore you can never trust any of them.
2. Managers know more than you do—or they *should* know more than you. That includes knowing how to do every job that is performed by those who work for them better than the actual employees.
3. Your supervisor has infinite time to pay attention to you. Anything you think important should be attended to—whenever *you* decide it's time for the supervisor to pay attention to it.
4. Managers can fix every problem.
5. Managers have all the resources in the world available to them, including money, to make improvements and fix problems.
6. Managers never have a bad day; they are never allowed to be in a bad mood, feel ill, or have a family or personal crisis.
7. Managers should never make mistakes or bad decisions.
8. Managers can read minds.

If you accept the first maxim for getting along with others—understand and respect the other person—then it is important for you to accept your supervisor for what he or she is. At the most basic level, your supervisor is just like you: a person who gets sick, has personal emergencies from time to time, has limitations (therefore makes mistakes), has feelings, and wants a decent quality of life. Treat your supervisor as you wish to be treated.

Supervisor Responsibilities

You and your supervisor have both similar and dissimilar job responsibilities and pressures. Here is a description of some supervisory responsibilities you may not know about to help set your expectations of your supervisor.

A Generic Supervisor's Role

1. *Ensure that work unit gets all assigned work done, meeting all schedule, budget, and quality requirements.* If the work unit performs well, the supervisor receives the credit along with the employees. If the work unit fails to measure up, the supervisor is usually the first to take the heat—no matter whose fault it is.

2. *Perform personnel and administrative duties, such as hiring and firing, performance appraisals, managing budgets, and assigning people to new tasks.* If this takes up a large percent of the supervisor's time, it can get in the way of the supervisor being able to focus on the work unit getting the "real work" done.

3. *Accomplish projects assigned by his or her supervisor.* No matter what level in the organization, supervisors receive their own tasks, ranging from technical tasks to leading the office United Way campaign.

Debunking the Myths

What is the significance of your supervisor's responsibilities to you? One of the most important effects is that your supervisor will probably have far less time to spend with you than you would like—a common complaint among new employees. To make the point even clearer, consider the following calculations:

1. The maximum amount of time a supervisor can spend, on average, with each employee equals the total hours in the work week divided by the number of the employees in the work unit.

2. If 40 hours is the standard week and 15 people work for the supervisor, then: 40 hrs. ÷ 15 people = 2.7 hours per employee each week.

Now subtract from the 40 hours some of those other responsibilities your supervisor spends time on:

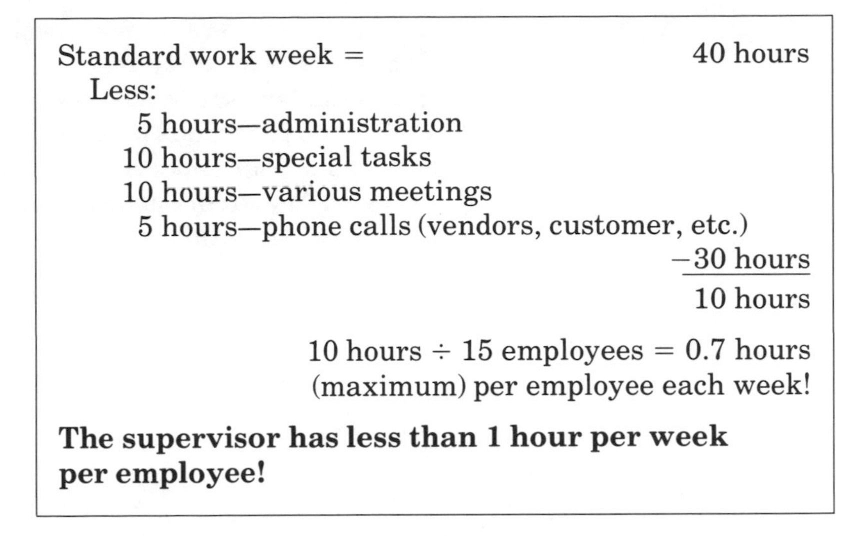

Standard work week = 40 hours
Less:
5 hours—administration
10 hours—special tasks
10 hours—various meetings
5 hours—phone calls (vendors, customer, etc.)
−30 hours
10 hours

10 hours ÷ 15 employees = 0.7 hours (maximum) per employee each week!

The supervisor has less than 1 hour per week per employee!

No wonder so many employees feel ignored!

Supervisor Authority

The other key point to remember is that unless you work for the owner or president of the company, your supervisor is the employee of a higher-level supervisor. Therefore, your supervisor may not be entirely free to make decisions on things such as resource allocations and expenditures, company policy, and strategic direction. Many employees become frustrated that their supervisors can't spend more money on computer equipment, won't change a company policy about taking leave, or don't agree to develop a new product line without approval from "higher up." Don't overlook the fact that your supervisor is simply unable to do these things because of constraints imposed by his or her supervisor. Just like you, your supervisor has been delegated a certain level of authority to make decisions. If your supervisor ignores these constraints and steps beyond bounds, he or she may receive a reprimand or even be dismissed from the company! Develop an understanding of what your supervisor really can and cannot do.

Understanding Your Supervisor

Your supervisor will have style preferences and behaviors that you will need to understand and adapt to. You must take the initiative to research how your manager operates. "Worksheet 1: Understanding Your Supervisor" is a set of questions that can help you to start assessing your supervisor's preferences. Your own observations will probably be sufficient to make this assessment. You may be able to get some of the answers from a coworker whose judgment you trust. There is a risk in relying on someone else to evaluate your supervisor—your coworker may react differently than you do to various behaviors. What bothers your coworker about your supervisor may not make a difference at all to you. Try to corroborate the opinions of others with your own observations.

Worksheet 1: Understanding Your Supervisor

1. My supervisor is most available
   ___ first thing in the morning.
   ___ around lunch time.
   ___ at the end of the day.
   ___ other. (describe) ____

2. My supervisor likes to receive information that is
   ___ detailed.
   ___ summarized.
   ___ contains backup analysis.
   ___ contains just conclusions.
   ___ other. (describe) ____

3. My supervisor likes to communicate
   ___ face-to-face.
   ___ via the phone.
   ___ via written messages.
   ___ via electronic mail.
   ___ other. (describe) ____

4. Regarding employee autonomy, my supervisor likes to
   ___ get involved in everything.
   ___ get involved only when the employee asks for help.
   ___ never get involved.
   ___ other. (describe) ____

5. Regarding office hours, my supervisor expects employees to
   ___ arrive early to work.
   ___ arrive no later than official starting time.
   ___ work late.
   ___ work on weekends.
   ___ take work home.
   ___ never take a long lunch.
   ___ work at any time, as long as all assignments get completed.
   ___ other. (describe) ____

6. The type of employee behavior that makes my supervisor the most angry is:

   ____

   ____

   ____

7. The aspect of my job that my supervisor considers most critical is:

   ____

   ____

   ____

Classic supervisor problems and solutions

No matter how much effort you put into understanding your supervisor, there will still be times when you will become frustrated with certain behaviors. Here are some classic supervisor problems and steps you can take to alleviate the situation.

1. *My supervisor is never around.*

Is there a certain time your supervisor is usually in the office (e.g., early in the morning, lunch, late in the afternoon)? Your supervisor's secretary can probably help you to find this answer. If there is a particular time, make an effort to stop by then. If that fails, make appointments to see your supervisor. Explain the purpose of the meeting and what you hope to get from your supervisor. Make sure you are well prepared for your appointment so you don't waste the opportunity.

2. *My supervisor flies off the handle a lot.*

Try to find out what causes your supervisor to fly off the handle. Can you eliminate it from the work environment? For instance, if your manager hates dealing with details, can you keep your reports briefer by preparing and sticking to an outline? If not, try to identify whether your supervisor's anger is personally directed at you. If it is, you should set up an appointment to get some feedback, using the techniques described in Chapter 6, "Performance Feedback and Compensation." If it's not directed at you, try to overlook it unless the situation becomes extreme. If the behavior is truly abusive, ask your human relations department, your supervisor's manager, or a peer of your supervisor for some guidance.

3. *My supervisor never tells me how I'm doing.*

Schedule an appointment and ask how you're doing. Use the tips described in Chapter 6. Supervisors sometimes overlook providing feedback if the employee is doing a satisfactory job. Nevertheless, you deserve to know how well you are performing.

4. *My supervisor takes credit for my work.*

Is this really so? Is it really appropriate for you to present your own papers or sign your name to all your output? Will you eventually get the credit in an appraisal?

5. *My supervisor doesn't communicate with me.*

Schedule appointments to obtain critical information. See if there are preferred ways your supervisor communicates (for example, not face-to-face but through E-mail). Find out what other ways you can learn needed information—for instance, from company publications and coworkers.

Behavior You Should Not Tolerate

Unfortunately, some employees find themselves working for supervisors whose behaviors should not be tolerated at all. You do have rights as an employee. Some behaviors you do not have to take include:

- discrimination of any type, including that related to gender, race, and age;
- harassment of any type, including physical, verbal, and emotional;
- illegal behavior, including requests for you to participate in shady or underhanded deals.

If you encounter any of the above behaviors you must take action. You have a number of options available to you depending on the severity of the supervisor's behavior:

1. You can confront your supervisor directly. In less severe cases, your supervisor may not realize that the behavior is offensive to you. For example, a male supervisor may not see anything wrong with calling a female employee "Hon." Simply telling your supervisor how you feel, honestly and firmly, could halt the behavior.
2. You can contact an employee-relations person or some other person responsible for mediating employee/manager problems. You can discuss the problem confidentially and determine an appropriate set of actions to take. Be prepared to describe the situation with specific examples to support your allegations.
3. You can seek outside assistance from a lawyer, government agency, or the police, depending on the situation and its severity.
4. You can look for employment elsewhere. Many people believe that the victims in these types of situations must fight for justice to prevent the same sce-

nario from happening to future victims. You must decide this for yourself. If you have doubts that you can make an ironclad case or you are just not up to the stress of resolving the issue, it may just be easier to walk away from the situation and get on with your life.

The focus of this section thus far has been on the first maxim of getting along with others in the office place. What about your responsibility to understand how your opinions and behavior affect those around you? Take this quiz, "Are You a Problem Employee," **(Exhibit 8.1)** to see if you have the potential to be a problem employee.

Exhibit 8.1.

Quiz:
Are You a Problem Employee?

1. *After seven months on the job, you believe that your performance warrants consideration for a promotion. You:*
   a. drop into your supervisor's office unannounced at 5 P.M.on a Friday evening and demand a promotion due to your good performance. You threaten to quit if no action is taken.
   b. make an appointment, stating the intended topic you want to discuss, and prepare your rationale according to the guidelines in Chapter 6.
   c. hint around about your desire to progress through the ranks of the company because you feel as if you're at the bottom of the ladder right now.
2. *Two weeks ago you asked your supervisor to set aside some time to go over a report you have drafted. She still hasn't scheduled a meeting with you. You:*
   a. send your supervisor daily reminders in the form of notes and phone messages that she has been remiss in scheduling the agreed-to meeting.
   b. initiate the communication by sending your supervisor a concise, well-planned summary of the issue you need to discuss and the ramifications of waiting much longer to hold your meeting.
   c. walk by your supervisor's office frequently, hoping she'll be reminded that she needs to talk to you.
3. *Your request to attend the national trade conference for your profession is rejected. You:*
   a. immediately go to your supervisor's manager and complain that you are being denied professional development opportunity.
   b. talk to your supervisor to find the specific reason why your request was turned down and see if there's room for negotiation.
   c. complain to your coworkers about the short-sightedness of your supervisor.
4. *You pride yourself on your writing skills, but you receive feedback from your supervisor that the memos you've written lately need improvement. You don't agree with the feedback. You:*
   a. argue with your supervisor. You never did respect your supervisor's abilities.
   b. listen carefully to the feedback. If you continue to disagree on certain points, you get a second opinion from an experienced, objective coworker.
   c. do everything exactly as you are told. After all, this is your supervisor.
5. *You know your supervisor doesn't like surprises, and therefore likes to stay informed of the progress of the employees' work. You:*
   a. are sure to leave frequent notes, voice messages, or drop by the supervisor's office with up-to-the-minute status of every task to which you are assigned.
   b. provide status of key events or issues for a couple of weeks. Then you set up a brief appointment with your supervisor to determine if the quantity and quality of the status is what is expected, or if you should provide more or less.
   c. provide the same amount of status as the more senior coworker sitting next to you and assume that if your supervisor needs more, you will be told.

Exhibit 8.1. (continued)

6. *You can't seem to get along or agree on any topic with the coworker sitting next to you, be it about smoking in the office or the format of the presentation that you are both assigned to. You:*
   a. ask your supervisor to mediate every controversy.
   b. try to resolve each issue yourself. For those unresolvable issues that are inhibiting work completion or quality, you present to your supervisor a concise description of the problem and a recommended solution, understanding that your supervisor owes the other employee "air time," too.
   c. do nothing. You don't want to appear to be a troublemaker.
7. *Your industry is in a slump. Your company announces a 12-month salary freeze. You:*
   a. take the opportunity at the next all-hands meeting to berate management, recalling the days when salary increases were large and frequent.
   b. talk to your supervisor candidly. You assess your personal situation as to your career aspirations and financial situation. You decide whether you should seek employment in a thriving industry.
   c. accept the announcement and are thankful you have a job.
8. *One of the salespeople in the XYZ Company from which you buy widgets tells you he is fed up with XYZ and its management and has decided to quit. He also confides in you all XYZ's "dirty laundry," including the fact that he can't see how it will be able to continue to produce the line of widgets you rely heavily on. You:*
   a. quickly alert everyone you see in the office that it sounds like XYZ is about to go under.
   b. try to collect some additional data to back up the salesperson's claims, then give your supervisor a factual heads-up.
   c. do nothing. It isn't really your responsibility to worry about things like this.

Scoring Key:
Each "a" answer score 5 points
"b" is worth 2 points
"c" is worth 0 points

"B" is the right answer in each example because the employee has taken the initiative to respond with a positive, planned approach. If you chose "A," you probably would irritate your supervisor with a behavior that could appear hostile or irrational. If you choose "C," your supervisor probably wouldn't find you a difficult employee, but you are not looking out for yourself and you are not demonstrating initiative.

Total Score:

0–10	May be letting supervisor take advantage of you.
11–30	A forceful yet considerate employee.
31 and above	A potentially obnoxious employee.

Coworker Relationships

The second important set of relationships you will have to manage is that with your coworkers. Successful relationships with your fellow workers will improve your chances of receiving needed information from them, completing shared projects with minimal friction, and generally making your day-to-day experiences in the office more enjoyable.

Coworker relationships usually take on two facets, professional and personal. The *professional* facet consists of the way you do business, the "unspoken" or sometimes spoken rules and courtesies observed so that everyone can function in a comfortable environment. It includes understanding and respecting seniority, finding and benefiting from mentors, and working successfully in teams.

The personal, or *friendship,* facet builds camaraderie and makes the office a little more fun. It also helps build a concern for one another and a deeper understanding of what makes one another tick so you can be more considerate on the job. Personal relationships are developed by going to lunch with coworkers, sharing a story over the proverbial water cooler, or going out for a drink after work. Keep in mind that some people are not comfortable sharing part of their private self with others in the office and therefore choose not to socialize. That is OK. If you see this in others, accept the fact that you will not establish a close relationship with everyone in the office. Do not exclude these people from the professional facets of the workplace. Your project may depend on them whether you know them well personally or not. If you are reluctant to reveal your personal side in the office, remember that some very real work gets done in social settings. You will have to place additional emphasis on maintaining professional relationships in other ways.

Office Hierarchies

When you enter the workplace, your position in the office is more than just the title and job responsibility to which you are assigned. Most offices have an undocumented office hierarchy which prescribes certain privileges to employees, depending on where they fall in the hierarchy. The hierarchy can be based on a variety of criteria, level in the company and time with the company being the more common. It is important that you learn the rules of your particular hierarchy. Refer back to Chapter 3 for some tips on deciphering your new environment. Five examples of rules in typical offices are included here.

Five Typical Rules in Office Hierarchies

1. Office space allocations depend on how high you are in the hierarchy: More junior employees are assigned the smallest space with the least privacy and no windows.
2. Employees with the most time with the company get to choose the dates of their vacations first.
3. The more senior the person the more special projects or "extra-curricular activities" they get assigned.
4. In some environments, the senior people get more "perks," such as invitations to parties or golf outings, receiving sports tickets, or getting a better parking place.
5. Some companies won't promote people to certain position levels until they are "mature enough."

Mentoring

Mentoring can occur any time an experienced employee takes an interest in helping a junior employee improve on the job. Mentoring can be a single event, such as receiving feedback on a particular presentation, or, in the more classic form, can be an ongoing relationship. Mentors can change over time, depending on what tasks you are assigned.

A lot has been written on the importance of finding a mentor in order to get ahead on the job. The problem is, you can't just ask someone to be your mentor. You can, however, encourage mentoring with these three behaviors:

1. Be receptive to the coaching you receive from more senior employees. Listen carefully to the feedback and evaluate whether it makes sense and if you can follow the advice. Thank the person for the input.

2. Demonstrate interest and enthusiasm for learning more about your job and how you can improve in it. Ask genuine questions and make use of the answers.

3. Perform as well as you can on the job. Mentors are giving up their time to coach their "mentees." Therefore, they want to see a return in their investment.

Teamwork

Teams are formed to get work done. Teams of architects and engineers work together to design a building. A team of secret-service men and women protect the president's life. A team of consultants develop a proposal for a new contract. Although you probably worked on group projects in college, chances are you did not work as a team in the sense the work environment demands. Just like a sports team or an orchestra, all members of a work team are expected to pull their weight to contribute to the team's end goal. There is an interdependency of tasks assigned to each member. Success or failure belongs to the entire team, not to the individual.

If you are not accustomed to working as part of a team, there are two aspects of teamwork that are apt to give you difficulty. The first is getting used to the team receiving recognition for its accomplishments rather than your receiving individual recognition. If you are a successful team member, your talents will be recognized and you will find yourself selected to participate in other teams. Being a good team player is a skill on which you will probably be evaluated. Teamwork is becoming the norm in many companies. Your ability to perform in a team may become a part of your performance appraisal criteria.

The second aspect of teamwork that will challenge you is learning to work comfortably and cooperatively with people who are different from you. For example, in school most of your fellow students were roughly the same age, probably had close to the same grades from high school, and had similar motivations about studying to get a good job after graduation. In the workplace, you will see much more diversity in your coworkers. Now your fellow employees may:

- be at different points in their career (A person near retirement may have less ambition compared to you.);
- have different motivations for working (One person may be driven to make as much money as possible while another may be inspired to produce the best quality output possible.);
- be stressed about different personal events (Births, deaths, the challenges of raising children, and financial difficulties can all contribute to on-the-job performance.);

- prefer different work styles (One person may be a bold decision maker, another one cautious. One may like to work conceptually, another prefers details and specific tasks.);
- possess different abilities (One person may be able to easily envision a new project and lay out all the initial plans for it, while another may be much more skilled at implementing the details of the project, while not missing cost or schedule targets.).

You may grow impatient with coworkers who are different, especially in the areas of motivation and skill. Try to see how the differences can become assets to your project. Also, spend time starting to learn about your work style preferences. Could your preferences be annoying to someone else?

Personal Facets

Inevitably, after working with the same people for a while, you will begin to see a different aspect—the social and personal side of your coworkers. This is not unprofessional—in fact, developing personal friendships with coworkers can help make the job easier to accomplish and a whole lot more fun, too.

As with everything else, there are pitfalls to be avoided as your social/personal side comes out. You must be conscious of the degree to which you allow your social/personal side to enter the workplace.

Your Personal Life

Some sharing of your personal life with coworkers is positive—such as discussing buying a new car or house, sports, or movies. These topics generally evoke interest and even advice from coworkers. A small dose of this over lunch or at the coffee machine is acceptable and to be expected.

Some people take it too far. Watch it! Taking it too far means that an excessive amount of time and detail is spent on these topics or that the topics are too personal for the office. For example, no one wants to hear about every play made in your softball game last night, or every scene from the latest movie you saw. Besides the fact you're probably boring your audience, you are likely to be leaving the impression that you are either very self-centered, not busy enough at work, or not focused on the tasks assigned to you. And blabbing to everyone about your love life, family fights, or a medical problem is inappropriate. Save these discussions for close friends.

Office Romances

Many people vow they will never date anyone with whom they work. Others manage to successfully maintain parallel professional and romantic relationships. You have to decide what is right for you, but consider the following:

1. The number of dating situations that end in a breakup far outweigh the number that result in a lasting commitment. Breaking a relationship can get ugly—cruel words may be exchanged, biased opinions of the other person may be shared with coworkers, you may never want to see each other again. What happens when you have to keep working together? How do *your* relationships typically end? Is it worth the potential negative impact on your job success?

2. Known office relationships often become a hot topic on the office grapevine. Your relationship is suddenly in a fishbowl. Do you want to endure the scrutiny? Can the relationship withstand it?

3. Some companies have a policy that their employees may not date each other. While this may not hold up in court if you were fired for dating one of your coworkers, you still may be leaving a negative impression with key management.

Having an intimate relationship with a coworker is a risky venture. If you choose to pursue one, your best course of action is to be extremely discreet about it. Proceed with caution!

Sexual Harassment

Sexual harassment in the office has received a lot of attention in recent years. What constitutes sexual harassment is in the eyes of the beholder—an off-color joke, a Chippendale calendar, and physical touching have all been defined as sexual harassment.

Are you an offender? Hopefully not, although unintentionally you may be. Stay out of trouble with these steps:

1. Self-assess:
   Evaluate your words, actions, and surroundings for anything that might be even questionably offensive. Remember that the joke you find funny, the overly personal question you're dying to know the answer to, or the amusing poster you had in your sorority or fraternity house might be considered harassment to someone else. Find and eliminate the problem before someone else does.

2. Watch reactions:
   The joke you just told didn't go over so well? The chummy arm around your coworker's shoulder provoked a cringe? Often it's not too difficult to read that you've been offensive.

3. Don't ignore feedback:
   Whether it's a subtle comment about your calendar or an accusation from your coworker, take the feedback seriously because people lose their jobs now for sexual harassment.

Are you a victim? Again, hopefully not. If you are, these steps will be helpful:

1. Self-assess:
   Are you inviting the treatment you receive? Though sexual harassment is never pardonable, flirtatious behavior or provocative clothing may be considered an invitation for sexual come-ons. Many young women, in particular, are surprised when their overly short skirts or low-cut blouses evoke comments from their male coworkers.

2. Provide feedback:
   Often sexual harassment is truly unintentional. Some people are "touchers" with no sexual intentions whatsoever; others use terminology which they don't realize is offensive. Because the charge of sexual harassment is now very serious, tell the person who you consider to be harassing you how you feel and see if the situation improves.

3. Seek assistance:
   If providing feedback doesn't remedy the situation or if the harassment is severe, find a person you trust who can help you stop the harassing behavior. Your manager, a human-resources representative, or other senior person can help you identify what steps you need to take. Be prepared to provide specifics about the incident or incidents. Explore how you can keep the matter as confidential as you need to feel comfortable. While this may be an embarrassing situation for you, don't ignore the problem. Your work performance can be detrimentally impacted if persistent harassment eats away at you with no resolution in sight.

There are many other behaviors you may either encounter in your coworkers or exhibit yourself that can strain your working relationship. Take the following quiz, "Are you a Problem Coworker?" (**Exhibit 8.2**) to find out if you have the potential to be a problem coworker.

Exhibit 8.2.

Quiz: Are You a Problem Coworker?

1. *After seven months on the job, you believe that you deserve a larger cubicle with a window because of your excellent performance on the job, even though you don't have the seniority needed. When one becomes available, you:*
   a. start moving your things into the cubicle immediately—after all, possession is nine tenths of the law.
   b. ask if seniority is the only criteria for getting such a cubicle. If not, make your request through the proper channels. If it is, lobby with your coworkers to change the criteria for allocating cubicles to include other factors.
   c. from now on, ignore the coworker who gets the cubicle through seniority alone.
2. *Your teammates keep missing deadlines, thus affecting your ability to meet your milestones. You:*
   a. immediately run to tell your supervisor exactly who is causing you to miss your deadlines.
   b. initiate a conversation with the teammates who are causing the problem to explain how you are affected, and explore what can be done to fix the problem.
   c. complain to your friends in the office about your teammates' inconsiderate behavior.
3. *A senior member of your team offers to stay late and help you with your project. You:*
   a. refuse any help because you feel you know what you are doing.
   b. remain after work to take advantage of the help, asking as many relevant questions as possible, and thanking your coworker before going home.
   c. accept the offer but end the session as soon as possible so you can enjoy your evening.
4. *You always studied while listening to your favorite rock group and would like to continue this practice at work. You:*
   a. bring in a radio/CD player and start using it during the day.
   b. ask coworkers if they mind if you bring in a radio/CD player if you use headphones to reduce the noise level.
   c. do nothing but tell everyone at every opportunity how much you miss having music while you work.
5. *Your product team must meet a deadline of tomorrow morning at 9:00. Everyone will be staying late to complete the project but you have tickets to the final game of the World Series. You:*
   a. leave on time knowing that your teammates understand how much you love baseball.
   b. explain the situation to your teammates and then work through dinner and miss the first two innings before you rush off to the game.
   c. cancel your plans but contribute very little to the project because you are so depressed.
6. *A coworker is having trouble finding information in response to a routine customer request and asks you for help. You are behind on several commitments yourself so you:*
   a. yell at your coworker about her incompetence and then find your manager so you can complain about being interrupted.
   b. help her respond to the customer and then offer to teach her during the lunch hour how to find the information herself.
   c. do nothing at the time but give your coworker the cold shoulder for being so inconsiderate to you.

Exhibit 8.2. (continued)

7. *Your new office-mate puts up a calendar with scantily-clad members of the opposite sex. You:*
   a. call the human relations department immediately and lodge a formal complaint.
   b. talk to your office-mate candidly about how you feel. You firmly explain you find the pictures offensive and want the calendar removed.
   c. say nothing to your office-mate but continue to fume every time you walk into the office.
8. *You and a manager are attracted to each other and begin to date. You:*
   a. tell everyone about your romantic dates and never stop talking about your new love interest.
   b. decide to pursue your relationship on evenings and weekends, being careful to limit your discussion with coworkers to neutral subjects.
   c. sneak around with this manager every lunch hour, meeting at various restaurants so you won't be seen. Deny everything when a coworker asks if you are dating someone in the office.

Scoring Key:
Each "a" answer score 5 points
"b" is worth 2 points
"c" is 0

"B" is the right answer in each example because the employee has taken the initiative to respond with a positive, proactive, planned approach. If you chose "A," you probably would irritate your coworkers with behavior that could appear hostile, irrational, or inconsiderate. If you chose "C," your coworkers probably wouldn't find you a difficult coworker immediately. If you continue to maintain a distance in both the professional and personal aspects of coworker relationships, however, your relationships and job performance will suffer over time.

Total Score:

0–10	Your lack of initiative and positive response to issues and problems will break down your relationships with coworkers over time.
11–30	A forceful yet considerate coworker.
31 and above	You may already be considered an obnoxious coworker.

Summary

This chapter has addressed two of the most important relationships you need to successfully manage in the workplace. There are others, such as those with secretaries, customers, or vendors, that will also be important. You will be successful if you apply the two basic relationship maxims to these relationships:

1. Understand the other person—then have patience and respect for him or her.
2. Understand how *your* opinions and behavior affect those around you.

Successfully managing all your office relationships is as important to your on-the-job success as accomplishing assigned tasks competently. Invest the time in managing your office relationships.

PERSONAL SKILLS

Section IV

Keeping Your Personal Life in Order

9

Introduction

Few people can completely separate their personal and work lives. Your non-work activities, social and family relationships, and general health and financial concerns can affect your performance at work. Personal concerns can affect your concentration, energy level, mood, and attitude. These in turn can positively or negatively affect your performance. This chapter suggests ways to maintain a balance between your work life and your personal life. Chapter 10, "Keeping Your Finances in Order," addresses how to avoid financial difficulties.

Maintaining a Balance Between Work and Personal Lives

A few lucky people have no trouble keeping their personal and work lives separated. At work, they focus completely on the task at hand, never thinking of the argument they had the previous evening with their significant other and ignoring the cost of recent car repairs. When away from work, they devote their time to personal matters. They leave work-related problems at the office. This is a healthy habit to cultivate but one that can be difficult to achieve. If you find yourself lying awake worrying about the report that's due next week or thinking about a personal problem during an important meeting, here are some suggestions that may help.

Are You Balanced?

Monitor how much time you are devoting to the work-related and personal aspects of your life. If you spend your work day making personal calls, listing all the things you'll do on the weekend, and watching the clock, reevaluate the purpose and value of work in your life. Perhaps you need a more challenging assignment or position. Perhaps you are in the wrong job or field. Perhaps you've lost sight of how you pay for your weekend activities!

If, on the other hand, you consistently work twelve-hour days, seven days a week, can't remember the last time you went out with friends, and haven't a clean article of clothing to wear, consider whether those extra hours at work are truly productive. Perhaps you need to learn how to manage your time better. Perhaps you have fallen into the trap of believing that workaholics are the only people who get ahead. You too may be in the wrong job or field. If you truly need to work excessive overtime for long periods of time to perform your regular duties, you may not have the skills or experience needed for your position. You may have to find a job more suited to your current ability level. Obviously the scenarios described above are extreme cases. If you recognize some of your own behaviors in either of them, you need to return to a more balanced lifestyle. Sometimes it is necessary to work long hours. Sometimes personal issues will creep into your work life for several days. Allowing either to happen for long periods of time will result in stress and reduced productivity.

Set Weekly Goals for Personal and Work Life

Take 15 to 30 minutes weekly to determine your personal and work goals for the coming week. Include a variety of goals. Some should be "fun" things, such as learning new skills, social activities, and athletic pursuits. Others will address chores and responsibilities. When you have arrived at your goals for the week, give the most important in each column a rank of 1, the second most important the rank of 2 and so on. Use the worksheet that follows, "Weekly Personal and Work-Life Goals Worksheet" to help.

Weekly Personal and Work-Life Goals Worksheet

Priority	Work Goals	Priority	Personal Goals

Once you have set some weekly work and personal goals, you must manage your time to accomplish them. Use the rankings of your goals to set your priorities. Schedule the higher-priority goals first and fit the other items in as you have time.

At the end of the week, review what you have accomplished from both your work and personal goals list. When reviewing your accomplishments, don't concentrate on what didn't get done. Instead, take pride in your successes, large or small, in both arenas. Don't use these lists to schedule every minute of your life. No one wants to feel the additional pressure of self-imposed schedules. Over a few weeks, identify trends in tasks that don't get done. Are you putting pressure on yourself to accomplish tasks that are unimportant or unnecessary? If so, allow yourself to focus only on your high priority goals. Do you see from reviewing your lists that you avoid tasks that you don't like to do? If so, explore alternate ways for you to get these items accomplished. For example, is there a leaky faucet or other item in need of repair in your home that you keep procrastinating about fixing? Sometimes it's worth the money to pay someone else to come fix it for you.

Replace Worry with Action

Rather than worry about a personal or work-related problem, take some action—no matter how small—to solve it. If you need a new car, starting bringing your lunch every day and save the money you would have spent in restaurants. If you're lying awake thinking about the report that's due, get up and write down ways you can improve it or make a "to do" list for the next day to ensure you make progress on the report. If all else fails, you could even go into the office and work on it. You weren't sleeping anyway! Taking some action can make the largest problem less worrisome and more manageable.

Use Commuting Time to Refocus

Whatever your mode of transportation to and from work, use the time you spend commuting as a transition period. Redirect your focus from one aspect of your life to another. On the way to work, think of the day ahead, leaving personal matters behind. On the way home, concentrate on important personal things. Many people find that their best ideas for how to tackle work and personal issues come during this transition period.

Maintain the balance between your personal and work lives by:

- Setting goals and priorities each week
- Monitoring the time you devote to each aspect of your life
- Acting to find solutions to problems rather than worrying
- Refocusing on the way to and from work

Hints for Personal Time Management

Everyone knows someone who seems to be able to get much more done than the average person. While many of these people have higher-than-average energy levels, many have also discovered ways to make the most out of their time each day. Here are some tips for squeezing more out of your day for personal time management.

Because work takes up so much of our waking hours Monday through Friday, at first glance it appears that the only time available for personal activities is in the evenings or on the weekends. Consider these ideas for finding alternative times to tend to your personal life and maximizing the efficiency of your time.

Use your lunch hour to do errands.

Bring your lunch from home and save both time and money.

Take advantage of the hours before and after work.

Many businesses open very early and close late to accommodate working people. Shop for non-perishables before work and drop off your dry cleaning. Some medical facilities also have extended hours so you can avoid taking time off work. Schedule appointments well in advance so you can take advantage of evening and weekend hours.

Use the commute-time going home.

The time you spend going home from the office does not have to be wasted time. If you drive, you can catch up on the news by listening to the radio or "read" books by listening to them on tape in your cassette player. Keep a notebook in your glove compartment to write grocery lists when you are stuck in traffic that doesn't move. If you ride a train or bus, you have even more opportunity for catching up on correspondence, doing needlework, or even taking a nap so you can stay up later for other tasks on your list.

Use pickup and delivery services.

Service businesses, such as dry cleaners, offer pickup and delivery right to the office with competitive prices.

Use one-stop stores and shopping centers.

Between your home and work there are probably one or more shopping centers where you can complete several tasks conveniently. Find these centers and organize your errands around a single stop.

Get up one hour earlier or go to bed one hour later.

You can gain seven useful hours a week by spending one less hour sleeping. This will not work for some people who require a specific amount of sleep. If you wake up tired, however, it may be because you are getting too *much* sleep, rather than not enough. Try this for a week to see if it works for you.

Free your weekends from housework for other activities.

If your social life is suffering from lack of time, do one hour of housework or laundry each weeknight to free you from the "weekend blues." Another option is to look into a housekeeping service. Many are very affordable.

Hints for Work Time Management

To better manage your time at work, read Chapters 4 and 5. Knowing what you are expected to do and creating a good plan to follow will save you significant time. Other ways to improve your use of time at work are:

Know your peak performance time and use it wisely.

If you don't come alive until after 10 A.M., use the early morning hours to return phone calls, clear paperwork off your desk, and perform other tasks that do not require your peak concentration. Conversely, morning people should save these tasks for later in the day when they are starting to tire. Use your peak performance hours for those tasks that require the greatest thought, creativity, and mental alertness.

Limit office socializing.

Although it is important to maintain good relationships with your coworkers, people often waste the first hour of the day in idle conversation. Bow out in a friendly manner after a few minutes.

Keep business calls short and to the point.

Talking on the telephone has become a national recreational activity. Business calls should not include more than a few social amenities before you settle down to the business at hand. When calling coworkers who tend to chat, arrange to have lunch or meet them after work for socializing instead of using the office phone.

Keep meeting attendance under control.

Meetings have been called the bane of American business. They frequently are poorly planned and run, resulting in several people being "held hostage" for significant portions of the day. In addition to following the advice in Chapter 7 when planning and conducting your own meetings there are several ways you can keep your meeting attendance under control.

Determine ahead of time whether you personally must attend the meeting. Sometimes the wrong people have been invited to a meeting. Sometimes you and your coworkers can agree that only one of you needs to attend and inform the others of the outcome.

Come in early or leave late.

In addition to helping you avoid traffic jams, coming in early or staying late can give you the quiet time you need to complete important tasks. With coworkers gone and no phones ringing, you may be able to accomplish a significant amount of work in only one extra hour a day.

Use the commute-time coming to work.

Just like the commute-time home, going to work can be spent getting ready for the day ahead.

Dedicate a portion of the weekend to work.

There are times when weekend work is unavoidable. Spending a few hours at the office on the weekend may be all you need to catch up on a critical project. If you arrive early, you will still have most of the day to enjoy.

Manage your time by:

- Changing inefficient routines at home and work
- Matching activities to your energy level
- Finding extra minutes in your day

Handling Significant Personal Problems

Every worker is faced at some point with a significant personal event, such as marriage or a serious family illness. Significant events may demand some of your time during working hours, require frequent or prolonged absences, cause you emotional or physical pain, or consume mental energy you usually apply to your work. Supervisors are not heartless automatons. Most know how much effort goes into planning a wedding or buying a house. If you let them know about significant events in your life, supervisors will seldom have a problem if you spend a few minutes on the phone arguing with the florist or tracking down a credit problem.

Although you should tell your supervisor about the really significant events in your life, do not share every personal crisis that occurs. A supervisor is not a parent substitute or close personal friend. When your latest romantic involvement falls apart, your car dies, or your cat gets sick, you need not tell your supervisor the details. Instead, carefully monitor your concentration and work performance whether you are experiencing a major problem or just a series of small personal problems. Talk to your supervisor if, after trying the stress relievers discussed later in this chapter under "Physical and Mental Health," your performance continues to suffer.

If you are spending *all* of your time conducting personal business at the office, your supervisor is bound to lose a sympathetic attitude. You have a responsibility to keep up with your workload. This is what the company is paying you to do. Come in early, eat at your desk, and stay a little later and you should have no trouble making a few personal calls during business hours. However, do not make personal long-distance phone calls at the company's expense. Have people call you, if possible, or get a phone credit card so the bills can be sent to you.

More serious personal problems may require you to take time off. To the extent possible under the circumstances, give your supervisor as much notice as you can. If your absence will affect a critical deadline, consider offering to work late or on the weekend upon your return. Your supervisor will appreciate your loyalty and dedication as will your coworkers who will be expected to cover for you during your absence.

Handle your personal problems by:

- Keeping your supervisor abreast of major personal events
- Making up time spent at work on personal business
- Scheduling time off for personal business in advance, whenever possible

Good Habits for Staying at Peak Performance

Ever notice that some people rarely have the performance problems experienced by others? They hardly ever get sick, always have energy, don't lose their cool in stressful situations. Certainly these people are lucky to have good genes and strong mental dispositions. If you look harder though, you'll often find that these people have developed good habits that help to reinforce the strong minds and bodies they were born with. Here are a few suggestions for good habits for you to practice.

Maintain Physical and Mental Health

Maintaining your physical and mental health will benefit you personally in both the short and long run, as well as improving your productivity at work. There are simple steps to follow for good health.

Eat a balanced diet.

You probably can recite by heart all the basic nutritional advice you have heard for years from family, teachers, and the media. You must choose whether or not to follow it for your own well-being. Make it fun! Learn to cook! If you live alone, take the time to be good to yourself by preparing and eating a healthy dinner. If you hate cooking, make lunch in the cafeteria or at a restaurant your main meal of the day; eat a lighter, healthful meal at home in the evening. Share the cooking chores, if you can. Some easy, healthy cookbooks are given in the Bibliography.

Get enough rest.

Getting enough sleep every night is part of adjusting to a regular work routine. Catching up by sleeping excessively on the weekends does not work.

Participate in regular exercise.

Whether you choose bowling, basketball, or badminton, the key to physical fitness is to do *something* regularly.

Not only is regular exercise good for you physically, it is one of the best stress reducers known. Team sports offer an opportunity to socialize, as well as exercise. Individual exercise can be done at your convenience and is a chance to restore your emotional equilibrium in solitude after a trying day. Even if you hated gym class, there is a sport or form of exercise out there that you can enjoy. Try something different! Rafting? In-line skating?

Avoid smoking, heavy drinking, and, of course, illegal drugs.

You've probably heard enough about the detrimental effects of cigarettes, alcohol, and drugs on your physical well-being in the short- and long-terms. You must decide yourself if the regular use of these substances is worth the potential results.

Maintain your good health by:

- Eating a balanced diet
- Getting enough rest
- Exercising regularly
- Avoiding cigarettes, alcohol, and drugs

Manage stress

If you follow the basic steps to good health, you will find that day-to-day stresses are minimized for you. If you know from past experience that you do react poorly to stressful situations, plan small mini-vacations throughout the year so you can get away from the stress. Some people save one or two vacation days for those unanticipated times when a day off is needed to recharge their batteries. Talking problems out with close friends or family is also very therapeutic. There may be a time when personal or work problems are so overwhelming that you need professional help. Recognizing that most people need it sometime in their lives, many companies provide confidential, professional counseling for their employees. Not only do they provide counseling for emotional problems, companies will also help with more serious problems, such as excessive drinking or drug use. There is no stigma associated with using such services. Companies consider counseling a good investment in a valuable resource—you!

Recognizing when you need to talk to your supervisor and ask for counseling sounds easy, but because of fear or embarrassment you may deny you need help. Your supervisor, observing the decline in your productivity, will have to bring the matter up with you. Your first instinct may be to continue to deny that anything is wrong. If you maintain this position, the company may decide to dismiss you for poor performance. You have a responsibility to yourself and to the company to cooperate in solving these kinds of severe problems. If you do not wish to use company-sponsored counselors, many health insurance plans will cover visits to private mental health professionals. Do get the help if you need it.

Manage stress by:

- Maintaining your health
- Planning time off to relax
- Getting counseling from friends, family, or professionals

Company Benefits

When employees first start out at a new company, they are usually hit with endless information about the benefit options available to them. Some benefits are automatically provided by the employer; others may be obtained at a reasonable cost to the employee. Since you may not have a lot of time to make decisions about which benefits you will choose, it helps to be familiar ahead of time with options you can expect from most companies. The following pages discuss commonly found benefits.

Understanding Your Health Benefits

Many of the benefits provided by companies are directly related to physical and mental well-being. We will explain the more common types of health-related benefits. Your company may provide additional health resources such as membership in fitness clubs, an on-site gym, or even child care to help relieve the strain of working and parenthood.

Health Insurance

You cannot do without some form of health insurance. If it is offered by your company, sign up for this benefit immediately, whether or not you have to contribute to the cost. More and more companies expect their employees to contribute to the cost of the insurance policy, as well as pay a deductible amount and a percentage of medical expenses which are incurred. Few policies will cover preexisting conditions.

If your company does not provide health insurance as a benefit, join a professional, fraternal, or academic organization which offers its members access to a group plan. These group plans can be less expensive than individual health insurance. Consider joining a health maintenance plan, which will cover preventive care, as well as illness. For as little as two dollars a visit, you can maintain your good health with a variety of doctors and health services. If you cannot find a way to join a group plan, you will have to obtain individual health insurance. Although individual policies are expensive, lack of health insurance can prove financially devastating.

Dental Insurance

Dental insurance, like health insurance, is offered as a benefit by most major companies. You may be expected to contribute a small amount to the cost of the policy, as well as pay a deductible amount and a percentage of the dental expenses. Some companies will not cover you until you have been employed for a year. If your company does not offer this benefit, your teeth are in good condition, and you can afford to maintain them with regular visits to the dentist, you may not need private dental insurance. Most expensive dental problems occur later in life. If you have already established a family, you may wish to find a private plan.

Eye Care Plans

Similar to dental insurance, eye care plans are usually offered by the larger companies. You will probably have to contribute to this benefit. Like dental care, eye care is usually a relatively minor expense for younger people.

Short- and Long-Term Disability Insurance

Financial advisors have found this type of insurance to be one of the most neglected areas of financial planning. No one likes to contemplate an illness or accident serious enough to disable you for extended periods or life. However, if faced with a disabling event, this type of insurance provides you with continuing income for some or all of the time you miss work. Note that disability income is usually less than 100 percent of your regular salary, but worth receiving nevertheless.

Drug and Alcohol Abuse Treatment

In response to the high incidence of drug and alcohol abuse in this country, companies often include in-patient and out-patient treatment for substance abuse in their benefits packages. Due to rising costs, the number of attempted treatments can be limited. If you need such help, take it very seriously and cooperate in your recovery.

Counseling

As mentioned earlier in this chapter, some companies provide counseling services for their employees. In addition, some will pay for private mental health services as well.

Bridging Health Insurance between School and Work

If you are still in school, investigate ways to maintain your current health benefits until you are covered by your employer. Even if you are as healthy as the proverbial horse, a single sports- or accident-related injury could cost you thousands of dollars. One young man broke his wrist playing softball the summer after college, while he was not insured. Complications brought the bill to over $9,000. Three years later he is still making monthly payments to the hospital and doctors to maintain a good credit rating.

Determine the conditions under which you are presently covered. Your parent's health insurance policy may cover you as long as you are a student or unemployed. Once you have graduated or taken a part-time summer job, you may be uninsured during the period before you start your full-time position. You may have to obtain a health insurance policy in your name, which can be rather expensive. Not having health coverage, however, can be even more expensive.

While still covered under your present policy, consider having dental and eye examinations as well as a physical. Your work policy may not cover preexisting conditions or may not start until you have been with the company for a specified period of time, often six months to a year. If you have a serious preexisting condition, try to continue your present coverage until you are covered by your policy at work.

Understanding Personal-Leave Benefits

There are many types of *personal-leave* benefits which provide you income when you are absent from the office for any of a number of reasons. Not every company offers every type. Smaller companies may have less formally defined leave policies.

Vacation

New employees usually have limited vacation time allocated to them. Sometimes they must wait six months to be entitled to their first week off. Seldom will they receive more than two weeks vacation in their first year. Vacation days, however, are given in addition to company holidays. Although you may be accustomed to long school vacations, you can adjust to this new vacation schedule by taking vacation days in conjunction with company holidays, thus extending your time off to meaningful periods for fun and relaxation.

Sick Leave

In most companies, employees are either given a certain number of paid sick days a year or they acquire them over time based on the length of employment. Paid sick leave is a *privilege*, not an employee *right*. Since this and other time-off benefits are part of the company's overhead, the costs come directly out of the company's profits. Employees who regularly use all their sick days are often viewed as unprofessional for abusing their privilege. Most companies closely monitor the use of sick time and other time taken by their employees. Your supervisor will probably speak to you if you are suspected of abusing your absence benefits.

We cannot specify exactly how sick you must be before you should stay home. Consult your physician for professional advice. As a courtesy to your coworkers, if you are ill with something which is contagious do not come into work and infect them.

Personal Business

Not every company has a special category of time off for *personal business*. This benefit, should you even have it, is specifically for conducting business that cannot be done outside of regular business hours. Attending house settlements or appearing in court are examples. A wise new employee will use vacation time, if available, instead. After building a good track record of attendance with the company, you may consider using this benefit as it was intended. Never abuse such a generous benefit. Always offer to come in early or stay late to make up for some of the time you have used for personal business. This gives the impression that you understand and care about the company's bottom line and it will stand you in good stead should a serious personal emergency ever arise.

Time off for a death in the family usually falls into the category of personal business. This benefit is usually restricted to the death of close relatives, such as parents, spouse, or siblings. Some companies do not pay you for this time but will allow time off without pay.

Jury Duty and Military Leave

Another category of leave is jury duty and military leave. Some companies will make up the difference between what you are paid for these activities and your normal salary; others will not. You will probably be expected to provide documentation to qualify for this benefit. Notify your supervisor of your impending absence as soon as you can.

Absences without Pay

If you need time off from work for a legitimate reason, such as a personal emergency, and have no leave benefit which covers the circumstances, you will have to negotiate time off without pay. If you have been keeping your supervisor informed of a developing personal problem or if the emergency is beyond your control, such as a death in the family, you should be able to take the time off with no future repercussions. If, however, you have a track record of frequent, unexplained, or unplanned absences, your supervisor may be reluctant to allow the time off. You have not established your personal credibility and now, in a real emergency, your request is suspect. Reliable attendance can be critical to establishing your professional reputation.

Summary

The interaction between your personal and work lives can have a beneficial or a detrimental effect on both. Balancing these two vital aspects of life requires both knowledge and skills. Setting goals, recognizing and relieving stress, maintaining good physical and mental health, and managing your time wisely will help you achieve this balance. The next chapter, "Keeping Your Finances in order," gives guidelines and tips for reducing personal stress from another source—your finances.

Keeping Your Finances in Order

10

Introduction

Learning about personal finances is not as difficult or complex as it seems. A little research on your part can result in significant financial advantages which can allow you to pursue other personal goals. There are three major reasons for you to learn about finances:

1. Understanding how you spend your pay will help you economize, allocate money for future goals and current expenses, and provide for unexpected events without going in debt, thus reducing concerns which may cause stress and affect your performance.

2. The earlier you begin to plan and save for the major financial milestones which lie ahead of you, the more money you can accumulate, almost painlessly, to meet your long-term goals.

3. Financial strategies should be developed and modified based on your individual circumstances. Relying on the methods used by your parents or older friends or siblings may not be beneficial to your particular situation.

This chapter starts by familiarizing you with some of your major financial considerations. To do this, you will use "Personal Finances Worksheet 1: Your Income" and "Personal Finances Worksheet 2: Your Expenses." It concludes with some tips for taking preventative measures to ensure financial stability throughout your life. Many financial magazines and books give more detailed practical guidelines for you to follow in planning your financial future. A list of basic financial references can be found in the bibliography.

Sources of Expenses

Your first paycheck! Before you run out to buy the little red sports car you have always wanted or lease an apartment you can't afford, you need to determine how much money you actually have available to you. You may be surprised by how much money you must spend on some necessary but less glamorous items. Four of the main areas that will eat up your paycheck are taxes, insurance/benefits, housing, and savings.

Taxes

What a shock it is to see how little you actually bring home to pay the bills! You may have been employed before taking your first full-time position so you anticipated the disappearance of taxes from your paycheck. Federal taxes and social security deductions (FICA) will probably be taken directly out of your pay by your employer. The amount is a predetermined percentage set by the U.S. government. The higher your salary, the higher the tax percentage which is applied. If you are now working in a different state or city, the amount of local taxes you must pay may be an unpleasant surprise. These will vary, depending on where you live. Local taxes can be a big surprise if they are not deducted directly from your check. For example, many communities have a tax on gross income (your total income before *any* tax deductions are made) which you are expected to pay directly to the community. It is *your* responsibility to find out how much you will owe, and if these taxes are not deducted by your employer, to have the funds available to pay them annually. Look in your phone book for your local departments of revenue and give them a call for assistance in determining how large your local tax bill will be.

Company Benefits and Insurance

Most companies offer a variety of benefits to their employees. Chapter 9 describes many of the commonly-offered company benefits. Often your employer will expect you to agree or to decline to participate in these plans on your first day of work. Do not be intimidated by all the forms. If the company picks up the entire expense and you are not asked to contribute in any way, of course agree to participate in these benefits. For other benefits which you must completely or partially pay for, ask how long you have to decide on each benefit. Often you will have up to 30 days to review what the benefit is and how much it will cost you. Taking the time to investigate the type and cost of company benefits will allow you to choose more wisely based on your individual circumstances and income. Ask questions of the personnel department or benefits-plan administrator. They are used to providing answers on these complicated issues.

Life Insurance

Unless you have dependents (a spouse, children, aging parents who you must provide for), this is an area where you can economize. If the company pays for the entire cost, there is no question that you should sign up for this benefit. However, if you must pay or substantially contribute and you have no dependents, your money would be better allocated to saving toward an emergency fund or paying for disability insurance. The only risk in not taking advantage of this insurance is that you could develop a condition which will not be covered if you apply for life insurance in the future. In general, unless you know of some genetic or other serious illness that runs in your family, this risk is small.

Pensions

It seems a little early to worry about retirement, doesn't it? With the recent changes in the pension laws, however, you can be entitled to a retirement benefit with as little as five years employment with the company. Although many people do change companies in less than five years, it is amazing how many stay five to seven years before making a career move, especially with large companies which have greater job flexibility. In light of the difficulties expected with social security fund distributions in the future, beginning to accumulate retirement funds as early as possible makes good sense. Certainly, if the company is paying for this benefit, you have nothing to lose.

If you are expected to contribute to the pension fund, determine how safe the types of investments your company uses for their retirement funding are and whether or not the program guarantees your benefits. Guaranteed benefits are found in what is termed a *defined* plan. A defined plan specifically defines the amount of pension you are entitled to based on the number of years you are employed with the company and your salary. Pension funds which invest in limited types of investments, in particular only in the stock of the company, are more risky than those which use a variety of investments.

Find out what happens to your contribution if you leave before you are *vested* (entitled to a future retirement benefit). If you are vested, you can choose to leave the funds where they are if you leave the company, and receive a retirement check directly from the company in later years. Sometimes you can *roll over* pension funds from one company to the next. This means your retirement fund can continue to build even if you leave the company. When deciding whether to leave your retirement funds with your current company or roll them into the pension fund of your next employer, consider the long-term financial stability of both of the companies and both of the funds. A final alternative is to withdraw your contribution (usually with the associated interest) and roll it into an Individual Retirement Account (IRA) with little or no tax consequences.

Housing

More and more people continue to live with or are returning to live with their family. The reason may be obvious if you have started to look for your own apartment or when you begin the budgeting worksheets later in this chapter. Housing is probably the biggest single expense you face. Many people are not willing to make the life-style adjustments needed to pay for their own place to live. If living with relatives is not an option for you, we provide some alternatives.

Choosing a location

When choosing a place to live, price is not the only consideration. If you are going to be working in an unfamiliar location, carefully determine the quality of the neighborhoods you are considering. The local police should be able to tell you the crime statistics for various locations. Ease of transportation to work is yet another consideration. Inexpensive housing which requires you to make an hour commute in heavy traffic may not be a bargain. The manager who hired you or your company's employee relations department may be a source of this kind of information. Talk to someone from the company who is willing to discuss your housing concerns but be aware that they may not always know where safe, convenient, inexpensive housing is located.

Using an agent

If you decide to use a real estate agent to help you, be aware that they usually work on commission from the owners who have units available for rent listed with the agency. They will not help you find a place to live which is not one of their listings. You may have to work with several agents before you find a suitable unit to rent.

Share living quarters

One way to reduce housing expenses is to share someone else's house or apartment. Agencies will match you with people looking for someone to share their home. They take into account life-style compatibility so you do not waste time interviewing with people who are likely not to work out for you. Fees for this service vary.

If you are hired by a large company, it is possible that they can put you in touch with other newly-hired people who would consider having a roommate. You may also be able to locate a roommate through a religious or other organization of which you are a member. Is there a university near your work? Graduate students frequently are searching for someone to share expenses. The university may have a formal roommate matching service or just a bulletin board you can search.

The advantages of moving in with someone who has a home or apartment to share are that they have already born the expense of security deposits, they may have kitchen equipment and furnishings which you can use, and your name is not on the lease or mortgage. You have no formal contractual agreement to meet. If it doesn't work out, you must only bear the expense of moving again. On the other hand, the location or accommodations may not be entirely to your liking. You may be unable to find a situation close to work or located near public transportation. You might not like sharing a bathroom with (essentially) a total stranger.

Find a roommate

Alternatively, you can rent an apartment or house of your choosing and then try to find a roommate. In this case, of course, you must have enough money to pay the equivalent of two to three months' rent in security deposits, as well as the first month's rent up front. You may not have furniture or money to equip the home. Finally, you are legally bound by the lease. If you cannot find a roommate immediately or some other crisis occurs in your life, you may lose your security deposit and/or be required to pay the landlord the full amount of the lease, whether or not you are living there. Getting rid of a roommate who turns out to be a problem is not always easy. Get an agreement in writing of the conditions under which you are renting to a roommate, including a clause for thirty-days notice (on both your parts) prior to the roommate moving or your asking him or her to move. Finally, before you sign the lease, determine if you *can* have a roommate. Some leases do not allow either roommates or subletting to someone else.

Savings

Investing $2,000 a year for ten years when you are in your twenties and NEVER saving for retirement again can result in a larger retirement fund than if you start saving $2,000 a year in your late thirties and save for 30 years. How can this be? It is not sleight-of-hand; it is the "magic" of compound interest and reinvesting dividends over long periods of time. If you are the type of person who can defer current pleasures for future gains, now is the time to save, save, save. Even if you are not that kind of person, reconsider making yourself save *something* regularly as a top priority. You can't turn back the clock when you need that money for a down payment on a house, tuition for your children, or retirement some time in the future.

Your company savings plans can make this easy by contributing matching funds, managing your investment without a fee, and providing for payroll deductions. If your company has a savings program, especially one to which they also contribute matching funds, seriously investigate and consider signing up for this option. In a matching funds savings program, the company contributes some percentage to your savings fund—for example, fifty cents for every dollar you contribute up to some set percentage of your salary. You must be careful, however. Many of these programs are part of retirement planning and cannot be withdrawn from without penalty until you are 59 and a half years of age. This may not be a good way to save for an emergency fund. A plan which has company stock as the only savings option can also be dangerous. If you get laid off, chances are the company stock will also have lost value. This is a risk you must balance against the amount of the company's contribution to your savings. Be sure you understand the terms under which you can get the money if you leave the company, for any reason.

Some companies offer you access to company credit unions. A credit union is a financial institution which pools the money employees save with them and lends it to employees at, sometimes, more favorable rates than those of regular banks. Many employees also appreciate the convenience of a credit union even if the rates are the same as other commercial savings and lending institutions. Check to see if your company's credit union is federally insured for amounts up to $100,000. Do not deposit your money with them unless they are, because you could lose your savings should the credit union fail.

Managing Your Money

Now that you have an understanding of the major expenses you will probably incur, you can develop a budget for managing your money. Defined most simply, your budget consists of two elements: your income and your expenditures. Your income must be equal to or greater than your expenditures in order not to incur any debt. As unpleasant as it might be to you, set up a budget and follow it.

Estimating Take-Home Pay

Your *gross income* per pay period is equal to your annual salary divided by the number of pay periods in the year. Unfortunately, this usually is not the amount of money you will see in each paycheck. To determine your *net income* or *take-home pay,* you need to know what deductions your company makes from your paycheck. Deductions generally include most of the expenses described earlier in this chapter:

1. Taxes: federal, state, possibly local, social security

2. Company benefits: various types of insurance you have selected

3. Savings: company savings plan, additional pension contributions, credit union Christmas clubs, etc.

4. Miscellaneous: charitable giving, employee club dues, etc.

Use the "Personal Finances Worksheet 1: Your Income" to estimate your gross pay and your paycheck deductions. If you are trying to determine how much rent you can afford on an apartment before you start your job, you can estimate your take-home pay in advance by calling the company payroll department. Ask what federal tax bracket you are in, what your state and local tax percentages will be, your social security deduction, and how to calculate the cost of the benefits you must pay for. The figures may not be exact, but will help you estimate how much money will be available for other expenses.

Personal Finances Worksheet 1: Your Income

Gross Salary	
Less Deductions:	
Taxes	
Federal taxes	
Social Security	
State taxes	
Local taxes	
Benefits/Insurance	
Medical insurance	
Dental insurance	
Eye care insurance	
Life insurance	
Disability insurance	
Other	
Savings	
Company savings plan	
Additional pension	
Other	
Miscellaneous	
Charitable giving	
Other	
Total Deductions	
Total Annual Take-Home Pay	

________________ ÷ 12 = ________________

Annual Take-Home Pay　　　　Monthly Take-Home Pay

Your Pay Period

Find out if your company pays weekly, biweekly, or monthly. This is your *pay period.* Many companies do not pay for the current pay period until the end of the following pay period. One of the biggest shocks the authors ever had was finding out the hard way that the first companies they worked for paid their employees twice a month *and* a pay period behind. That meant the work performed from July 1 through 14 did not result in a paycheck until the end of July! And that meant no money for the entire first month of employment. Try explaining that to your landlord! Don't make this mistake if you can help it. Ask about a company's pay policy so you can at least know what to expect and can plan ahead.

One more thing to consider about pay periods is that, depending on how long they are, they will not necessarily fall on the same dates each month so you will not always receive the same amount of pay each month. For example, if you are paid weekly, you could receive four paychecks one month and five paychecks the next month. Keep this in mind when planning your budget. You may have to put a little bit of some paychecks away to cover payments in the following month.

Estimating Your Expenses

The next step in planning your budget is to estimate what your monthly expenses will be. Use the "Personal Finances Worksheet 2: Your Expenses" to capture this information. Start by writing down all your estimated *fixed expenses* for a year that are not already deducted from your paycheck by your employer. Fixed expenses are those you must pay because you are required to by law, such as taxes, or through a contract you have made, such as rent or mortgage, car payment, school loans, and additional insurance.

Next add estimates for those things you have some control over, also called *discretionary expenses:* savings, utilities, food, clothes, medical expenses, recreational activities, and so on. Remember that utility bills may vary by season. Don't forget to include an estimate of your long-distance use, as well as the fixed part of the phone bill.

Personal Finances Worksheet 2: Your Expenses

Fixed Monthly Expenses:	
Local taxes	
Additional insurance (car, homeowners, etc.)	
Rent or mortgage	
Car payment (or other required transportation expenses)	
School loans	
Other loans	
Other fixed	
Total Fixed Expenses	
Monthly Discretionary Expenses	
Utilities (heat, water, trash, condo fees, etc.)	
Phone (local and long distance)	
Car maintenance and gas	
Additional medical (deductibles, co-payments, prescriptions)	
Savings	
Food	
Clothing (include laundry and dry cleaning)	
Charitable giving	
Entertainment	
Vacation	
Miscellaneous	
Total Discretionary Expenses	
Total Monthly Expenses	

Balancing Your Budget

Compare your monthly totals on both worksheets. If your monthly income does not cover everything in your budget, revise the discretionary figures until it does. As long as you have not committed to expensive housing or car payments, you should be able to devise a budget which includes savings and money for fun. Reserve about five to ten percent of your income to make up for estimation errors. You may not find an apartment which includes heat in the rent. You may have underestimated your long-distance bill if you have moved far from home for your new job.

You now have a monthly figure for each category. Set aside enough money in your bank account each week to cover your monthly fixed expenses. To determine how much you will spend on each category of discretionary expense, just remember not to exceed the total for discretionary expenses. If you splurge on a piece of clothing, you will have to cut back in another discretionary category that month to balance it out.

Beyond a Balanced Budget

You now have a balanced budget. This budget will ensure that you will not incur debt as long as nothing unexpected or disastrous happens. Here are some additional tips for enhancing your financial stability.

1. *Keep three to six months worth of net income readily available.*

Readily available means in a bank savings account or money market fund where you can immediately withdraw the funds without penalty. Why do you want to do this? Three to six months worth of net income in savings will help tide you over in the event that you unexpectedly lose your job. Three to six months is the average amount of time it takes a person relatively new in the work force to find a new job.

In order to achieve this, you will have to save—at minimum—an amount equal to your weekly net income multipled by 12 (weeks). To do this in a year, divided the target amount by 52 to arrive at a weekly savings rate. For example: If your weekly net paycheck is $400, you should have $4,800 in your emergency fund. To accomplish this in one year, you must save $92.30 a week. This amount may be daunting, but *do* save *something* every week toward this end.

2. *Save five to ten percent of your gross income.*

Financial experts generally suggest five to ten percent annual gross income savings as an achievable objective. This money can be used to attain lifelong financial goals, such as buying a home and putting children through college. It also provides additional financial resources when you retire. Where you put this money will depend on your financial goals. For example, if you want to be able to retire at age fifty and buy a yacht, you may have to consider aggressive investment strategies that offer greater opportunity to make money but also have associated with them greater risk of loss. The experts also recommend putting your money in a variety of investments—stocks and mutual funds, bonds, etc. Eventually, you may want to consult a professional financial planner to devise an investment strategy that's right for you.

3. *Minimize use of credit cards.*

No matter how alluring the offer of a line of credit is, credit cards should be used as a convenience only. Pay off the total amount you charged at the end of every month. If you can't, reexamine your spending habits and alter your budget. You are living beyond your means. Do use the credit cards from time to time, however. When you apply for a car loan or mortgage, your ability to show responsible use of a line of credit will be key to getting your loan application approved.

4. *Pay your school loan faithfully.*

The federal government is cracking down on those who default on school loans. Trying to avoid this responsibility can put your entire financial future and, in some industries your job in jeopardy.

Summary

Understanding how to manage your money requires knowledge and discipline. It is worth your time to gain this understanding. Secure finances will give you peace of mind and provide you greater spending flexibility later in life. In this chapter you learned how to create and stick to a budget and follow sound financial techniques. The next chapter provides the skills you will need to manage your career.

Section V

PUTTING IT ALL TOGETHER

Putting It All Together: Managing Your Career

11

Introduction
Take Control!

Just as other facets of your professional experience, successfully managing your career also requires initiative and advanced preparation. You may expect supervisors, mentors, or human resource personnel to look out for you and steer your career development. This is not the case. Although these resources may provide some guidance, you are the only person who knows enough about you, your interests, and personal goals to make these decisions. You are the only one who is completely motivated by your own self-interest and not that of the company. If you want to succeed as well as be happy in your career, you must assume responsibility for directing your own career growth. It's up to you and nobody else!

A Process for Career Development

Step 1: Set a Goal

In order to *manage* your career development, you must have an idea of where you want to go with your career. Without a career goal in mind, you could end up anywhere! Your goal could be a specific type of position, such as someday becoming the chief financial officer of a major Fortune 500 company. Alternatively, your goal could be to gain a set of experiences throughout your life, such as experiencing many different cultures around the world through various job positions. For many of us, defining a career goal is a difficult thing to do. It requires an honest understanding of yourself, uninfluenced by the pressures of family, friends, and societal expectations and definitions of success. There are several good resources available, including books and tests, to help you define your career goals. If you feel confused about where you want to go, it will be worth your while to seek out these resources.

Step 2: Evaluate Your Skill Set

Once you know where you are going, you need to determine how you are going to get there. Start with understanding where you are today. In this book's introduction chapter we discussed four factors which contribute to your performance in the workplace: personal characteristics, basic mental abilities, academically-gained knowledge, and work practices. These four factors form the basis for determining what skills and experiences you need to obtain in order to reach your goal. You first need to honestly evaluate your current strengths and development areas in each of the four categories. Use the "Career Management Worksheet: Self-Evaluation" to guide your process. Include in your answers both your own self-assessment and feedback you have received from your supervisor.

Career Management Worksheet 1: Self-Evaluation

	Current Strengths	Current Development Needs
Personal Characteristics (Such as positive attitude, ability to respond to change, integrity, self-confidence, ambition)		
Basic Mental Abilities (Such as problem solving, logic, analytical thinking, creativity, application of abstract or mechanical thought)		
Academic Knowledge (Such as accounting, engineering, computer, medical, architecture)		
Workplace Practices (Such as ability to decipher the organization, efficiency in grasping new assignments, planning skills, ability to work with others)		

More on Step 2: Your Personal Life

One additional factor you need to consider in Step 2 is your personal life. To be happy and get a sense of fulfillment from your work, you must maintain a balance between work and your personal life. If, for example, you do not like to travel, you will never be happy in a job requiring you to be on the road every week. Use the "Career Management Worksheet: Personal Preferences" to clarify:

Your style preferences. Do you like to be flamboyant and the center of attention or do you prefer to work quietly behind the scenes? Do you like to juggle several projects at one time or do you prefer to focus your attention on completing one project thoroughly?

Your limits. You don't want to travel a lot? You are limited geographically in where you will work because you want to be near family? You do not want to work on weekends?

Your life priorities. What is most important to you? Family? Religious faith? Community service? Political action?

Your motivations. Are you motivated by the sense of a job well done? Material wealth? Security? Power? Becoming an expert in one field? Maintaining a well-rounded life?

Career Management Worksheet 2: Personal Preferences

My style preferences:

My limits:

My priorities:

My motivations:

Step 3: Determine the Requirements for Your Goal

Now you need to better understand what is required of people who are doing what you think you want to do. Just as you defined your personal profile of skills and personal objectives, you need to define the skill and lifestyle profile of the position to which you aspire. There are many ways you can obtain this information. Some organizations have written job descriptions you can ask to see. Ask your human-resource representative, if you have one, for help. Extend the techniques you learned in Chapter 3 to learn about other positions in the company. Ask people who hold these positions to explain to you what they do. Find out what skills and experiences you must have to be qualified for their jobs. Ask what they like and dislike about their work to flesh out the advantages and disadvantages of the position. Find out about their career paths to learn about prerequisite experience for the position. If you think you might want to change companies or professions, apply the same techniques to learning about jobs elsewhere. You will find that this is one step in managing your career where most people will be very happy to help you.

As you gather this information, collect it in a format that can easily be compared to your personal profile. The next two worksheets, "Career Management Worksheet 3: Goal Requirements" and "Career Management Worksheet 4: Goal Preferences," will help you do this. It is important to identify what is necessary to achieve the target position, and what the advantages of the position are.

Career Management Worksheet 3: Goal Requirements

	Skills Important to the Target Position	**Skills Not Important to the Target Position**
Personal Characteristics (Such as positive attitude, ability to respond to change, integrity, self-confidence, ambition)		
Basic Mental Abilities (Such as problem solving, logic, analytical thinking, creativity, application of abstract or mechanical thought)		
Academic Knowledge (Such as accounting, engineering, computer, medical, architecture)		
Workplace Practices (Such as ability to decipher the organization, efficiency in grasping new assignments, planning skills, ability to work with others)		

Career Management Worksheet 4: Goal Preferences

Style preferences

Limits

Priorities

Motivations

Your final task in Step 3 is to compare your personal profile, both skills and preferences, to that of your target career goal. Which items on your lists match those on the target list? What's missing from your list? Are the missing profile items things that you can change or obtain? Be honest. If for example the position to which you aspire requires you to speak a foreign language with native fluency, can you really develop that level of proficiency or are the people holding the position you desire all foreign born and raised?

Step 4: Charting Your Career Road Map

With the understanding of the skills and experience you need to attain your career goal, you now need to develop a road map for obtaining them. A good first step is to look at the career paths of the individuals you talked to in Step 3 and the prerequisites for each of their jobs. You may find that you need to obtain an advanced degree, take additional college course work, attend company-sponsored training, or study certain subjects on your own before you can be considered for the position. You may be able to gain the job prerequisites in your current position by expanding the position. If you are unwilling to acquire the prerequisites, eliminate the position from your list.

What other interim positions can you think of that would help you obtain the same skills and experience? Write down all your ideas and put the potential positions in chronological sequence, where each job leads logically to the next. Make sure that the prerequisites for each job are met by the previous jobs in your plan. Remember: *The fastest path to your goal is not necessarily a straight line!* Sometimes you may have to make a lateral move to develop breadth of knowledge in addition to the depth of knowledge obtained from staying in one organization for a long time.

While you do want to keep a long-term goal in mind, focus the detailed planning of your career road map on the near term. Although you may have already decided that your ultimate ambition is to be a company vice-president, focus on positions which you can probably attain within a one to five-year time frame. Some of the positions you wish to pursue may be higher level jobs than you can move into immediately. In these cases, you will have to determine the intermediate positions to focus on to reach your goal position. Remember that a lot of factors can change as you progress through your plan.

Step 5: Evaluating Your Career Plans

The final step in the process of managing your career development is to evaluate your plans. Here are some sample questions you might ask yourself to determine the reasonableness of your road map:

1. Does the timing of your plan coincide with other planned life events? For instance, do you want to marry soon or later in life? Do you wish to have a large family right away or a smaller family later on?

2. Do you have the time, ability, and resources to attain the prerequisites you need?

3. Is your spouse, if you have one, in agreement with the steps and possible sacrifices needed to implement your plan?

4. Does the plan resemble the career paths of others who attained the desired position? Although your hard work could enable any plan to succeed, you can benefit from incorporating the successful experiences of others.

As you progress through your career, you will want to periodically reevaluate how reasonable and appropriate the plan remains for you. You may be surprised at how you have changed along the way. You may develop skills that you never dreamed possible. You may also find that your personal priorities change, especially after major life changes such as marriage, the birth of a child, or a severe family illness. When it is time to alter your plan, use the steps just described to again produce a career plan that works for you.

Making Your First Career Move

Many employees are anxious to move quickly up to the next rung of the career ladder, especially in their early years in the professional world. Too often, new employees seek or accept a new position before conquering all aspects of their present job. In doing so, they overlook the future value of developing in each of the four key areas—personal characteristics, basic mental abilities, academic skills, and workplace skills, both general and specific—before moving on to a new position.

Do not assume that you can pick up the missing skills along the way. As you progress in your career, the challenges in all these areas become greater for several reasons. You will be expected to have established the firm foundation we talked about in all these areas. More expertise will be expected from you and harsher criteria applied in evaluating your development needs. Less time will be allowed for developing any weak or missing skills. What started as a minor weakness can become a major liability.

Evaluating Your Current Position

If you think you are ready to move on, take time to critically assess whether or not you have truly mastered your present position and whether you have gained most, if not all, of the learning and experience available to you in this job. Use the following "Checklist: Are You Ready to Move On" to evaluate your present position for growth opportunities.

Checklist: Are You Ready to Move On

	Are there opportunities in your present position to:	Yes/No
1. Personal characteristics	• increase your understanding or appreciation of others? • expand your patience level? • cultivate a positive attitude? • continue to enhance or develop new personal characteristics which you value?	
2. Basic mental abilities	• solve challenging problems? • apply abstract or mechanical thought processes? • improve your logical analysis techniques? • develop creativity? • stretch your basic mental abilities?	
3. Academic training	• maintain and expand the academic training you have received?	
4. General workplace skills	• decipher the organization? • understand a new assignment? • plan and execute multiple tasks? • profit from appraisals? • improve your communications? • manage office relationships, while keeping your personal and work lives in balance?	
5. Specific workplace skills	• master critical areas of your job?	

Staying in Your Current Position

If you have answered "yes" to most of these questions in the checklist, your present position offers the kinds of growth experiences which will form a firm foundation for your future career advancement. Slow down and take advantage of the current growth opportunities available to you. Unless there are extenuating circumstances which make your current position intolerable, do not consider a new position if you have not essentially mastered your current job. An indication of whether or not you have mastered your position is when you can identify specific significant accomplishments you achieved in your position. Those above you know what mastery entails and will expect that you have a certain level of skills and understanding to apply to your next position.

Expanding Your Current Position

If you have answered "yes" to many of the questions on the checklist but have problems growing in *some* areas in your present job, there are ways you can initiate change without leaving your present position.

1. You can discuss your personal goals in these areas with your manager and determine how the job can be expanded to address your needs.

2. You can volunteer for activities which offer opportunities to improve those areas not covered by your present job. For instance, you can volunteer to chair a social-events committee, forcing yourself to become more adept at planning and conducting meetings, dealing with people outside your immediate unit, and sharpening your creativity.

3. You can set personal improvement goals, such as a 25 percent reduction in customer complaints or a 15 percent reduction in task-cycle time.

4. If your present position is not maintaining your academic skills, you can take a course outside of work or ask to be involved part-time in a more challenging project.

Moving Laterally Rather than Vertically

If you cannot expand your present position but still have developmental needs in the areas indicated, consider moving laterally rather than vertically. Find a position at the same level with different responsibilities rather than moving up the career ladder. This career strategy also provides more breadth than the common vertical move. Breadth combined with depth is a strength that can pay great dividends in the future. For example, if you have been a computer programmer on both manufacturing and financial systems, you may be more valuable in the long run than someone who has moved up quickly in the manufacturing ranks.

When You Need to Move On

If your evaluation of your current position yielded mostly "no" answers and your attempts to expand your position have failed, it is time to consider other options. Before you hand in your resignation, however, determine whether or not your present circumstances can be tolerated for a short period of time while you look for another position:

- If there are still one or two areas of development which the job offers, can you focus your attention on them while tolerating the lack of growth in the others?
- Are there opportunities opening up in the company in the near future for which you can prepare?
- Can you accept the limitations of your current position while searching within or outside the company for your next position?

Remaining employed while searching for a job has several advantages:

- It is far easier to find a job when you have one than when you do not.
- Prospective employers may question why you are unemployed. They may wonder if you are one of the "perpetually disgruntled," always searching for the perfect position, or they may suspect you were fired or laid off.
- You are in a better bargaining position with potential employers.

If you decide to resign, be sure you can afford to be unemployed for up to six months while searching for a job. Do this by creating the emergency fund discussed in Chapter 10 before resigning.

If Your Position is Wrong or Untenable

There are times when a position can no longer be tolerated:

- You may be severely underutilized in your position, learning few of the vital foundation skills you need for your future.

- You may not be performing adequately because there has been a mismatch between your skills and those required for the job. You may have loved class accounting exercises but find you hate your job creating monthly financial reports.

- Your supervisor may be abusive and the human relations department unwilling or unable to help you.

If you find yourself in such an untenable situation, finding another position becomes imperative. You can either seek a new position within the company or leave the company. Your company has a lot of time and money invested in your recruitment and training. Often a company will be willing to find another position more suitable to your skills or with a more compatible supervisor.

Initiating Your Move within the Company

Once you are confident that you have done your homework and you want to either expand your current responsibilities or move to another position within your company, set up a time to have a career discussion with your supervisor. A formal career discussion resembles a performance appraisal, although you will be more of an initiator during this discussion than during an appraisal. As in any job interview, you will be telling your abilities and qualifications. Your supervisor will be evaluating your proposal and sharing with you the company's expectations for your career advancement. Follow the steps below to manage your career discussion with your supervisor.

1. *Prepare for the career discussion.*

Before the career discussion, prepare to explain:

- *Why you wish to expand your current responsibilities or move into a new position.*
  Use your analysis of your current position, as described in the beginning of this chapter, to prepare this topic.

- *What you have learned about the positions which interest you.*
  Use the list of positions you have prepared and your evaluation of them in relationship to your work preferences and strengths and development needs.

- *How the change would benefit your career.*
  Use your analysis of long-versus short-term positions and the information you gathered on career paths of others.

- *Why you are qualified for the expanded responsibility or new position, or what you are willing to do to be qualified for it.*
  Use your understanding of the prerequisites for the job to justify your qualifications or define a course of action.

- *How the change would benefit the company.*
  Use your performance appraisal or a self-evaluation (see Chapter 6, "Performance Feedback and Compensation") to translate your accomplishments on your current job to potential performance in other jobs and positions.

2. *Set your attitude.* A career discussion is one more opportunity for feedback—both positive and negative—from which you can learn and grow. Come to the discussion with a positive attitude but be prepared for possible disappointment. During the career discussion, you may be told:

   - you are not ready to move to a new position or accept more responsibility;
   - you have not selected appropriate alternatives and positions for consideration;
   - you are not qualified or cannot qualify for a position;
   - no opportunities are available in the areas which interest you.

   News such as this is bound to be disappointing. Be prepared to listen, probe, and benefit from your supervisor's point of view.

3. *Take notes.* Listen carefully to everything your supervisor says and take notes. Your notes will help you put the feedback into perspective if some of it is disappointing.

4. *Get specific information from your supervisor.*

Just as you did during your formal appraisal, ask for specific examples of what your supervisor is telling you. If confronted with disappointing news, ask for the reasons why:

- you are not ready to move to a new position;
- you have not selected appropriate positions for consideration;
- you are not qualified or cannot qualify for a position;
- no opportunities are available in the areas which interest you.

If examples or reasons are not provided in enough detail for you to understand, probe by using phrases in your questions such as:

"Exactly what do I have to learn in order to move out of my present position?"

"In your opinion, what should my next career move be?"

"What else is involved in the position that I do not know about? Could you be more specific?"

"Could you explain the job responsibilities where I do not qualify?"

"What else do I need to do in order to qualify?"

"I didn't realize there were no growth opportunities in these areas. Can you explain the business reasons?"

5. *Prepare a plan of action if you and your supervisor agree.*

If you and your supervisor agree on a course of action for your future, outline what you need to do to prepare for the position or apply for it. If you need to prepare, ask for your supervisor's help in gaining the necessary skills and experience.

6. *Prepare a plan of action if you and your supervisor disagree.*

If you do not agree with your supervisor's evaluation of your proposal or the career plan the company has for you, you can pursue the subject with the human relations department. You can also have a career discussion with supervisors in other departments if they have positions which interest you.

If you are still not satisfied that the company offers you the career potential you seek, use the information you have gathered about positions in your field, your work preferences, and your strengths and development needs to find a job with another company.

When You Don't Get the Position

When you apply for a position within the company, you may be only one of several candidates considered. Understand this going in because, unlike receiving a private rejection from an outside company, you will have to continue to work with people who know you were denied the position.

You should receive an explanation of why you were not chosen for the position. If none is forthcoming, ask your supervisor for the details. Some potential questions to ask in this situation are:

> "In what ways were the other candidates better qualified?"
>
> "What can I do to improve my chances next time?"
>
> "Is there training available for a similar position?"
>
> "Are there courses I should be taking in night school to improve my qualifications?"
>
> "Can my current position be expanded so I gain more relevant experience?"

Just as in the appraisal process, your willingness to keep an open mind and listen carefully to the reasons for the rejection will benefit you. You will have more information for self-improvement and for selecting a more suitable position to apply for next time. Your gracious acceptance of the rejection and persistence in your current assignment will be seen as a sign of your maturity.

If You Leave the Company

If you find a position outside the company or, for whatever reason, are resigning, do not part ways by burning your bridges. Many people feel that their resignation offers an opportunity to unburden themselves about every grievance they have ever experienced on the job. Their resignation letter or exit interview with the human relations department is a singular display of rancor or complaining.

No one has a crystal ball with which to foresee the future. Remember that you may someday wish to reapply to the company or have to work with them in some other capacity, such as a vendor or consultant. Be mature and gracious in announcing your departure. Indicating that you have found another opportunity you wish to pursue is a good, safe manner to present your resignation. Always give the company two weeks notice of your departure. Be cooperative in documenting your current work and training your replacement.

Summary: Careers in the Future

Where once it was common to join a company, work exclusively for them and retire after forty-some years, workers entering the job market today are expected to change *careers* (not just companies) three to four times before they retire. To succeed under these circumstances, you must develop the foundation of workplace skills discussed in this book. In addition, your ability to take the initiative and control your own destiny will help you to thrive on the challenges you face through the 1990s and into the next century. When you take responsibility for your career rather than relying on others, you will find both a career path tailored to your individual aspirations and job satisfaction along the way.

Bibliography

Career Guidance

Build Your Own Rainbow
Barrie Hopson and Mike Scalley
Pfeiffer & Company, San Diego, CA, 1993

How to Choose the Right Career
Louise Welsh Schrank
VGM Career Horizons, Lincolnwood, IL, 1991

Joyce Laine Kennedy's Career Book
Joyce Laine Kennedy and Darryl Laramore
VGM Career Horizons, Lincolnwood, IL, 1993

What Color Is Your Parachute?
Richard Nelson Bolles
Ten Speed Press, Berkeley, CA, 1994

Computer Literacy

The Complete Idiot's Guide to PCs
Joe Kraynak
Alpha Books, A Division of Prentice Hall Computer Publishing
Carmel, IN, 1993

PCs Made Easy
James L. Turley
Osborn McGraw-Hill
Berkeley, 1991

Etiquette

Letitia Baldrige's New Complete Guide to Executive Manners
Letitia Baldrige
Macmillan Publishing, New York, 1993

Miss Manner's Guide to Excruciatingly Correct Behavior
Judith Martin
Galahad Books, New York, 1991

Finance

The Wealthy Barber
David Chilton
Prima Publishing, Rocklin, CA, 1991

More Wealth Without Risk
Charles J. Givens
Simon & Schuster, New York, 1991

Kiplinger's Personal Finance Magazine
The Kiplinger Washington Editors, Inc.
Editor's Park, MD 20782

Money (a monthly magazine available at newsstands)
Subscription inquiries:
Money
P.O. Box 60001
Tampa, FL 33660-0001

General

Excess Baggage
Judith Sills, Ph.D.
Penguion Books, New York, 1993
This book discusses how your strengths can become weaknesses and limit your potential.

How to Win Friends and Influence People
Dale Carnegie,
Pocket Books (Division of Simon & Schuster)
New York, 1981

Type Talk at Work: How the 16 Personality Types Determine Your Success on the Job
Otto Kroeger and Janet M. Thuesen
Delacourt Press, New York, 1988

Mathematics

All the Math You'll Ever Need: A Self-Teaching Guide
Steve Slavin
John Wiley & Sons, Inc., New York, 1989

Nutrition and Cooking

Better Homes and Gardens Quick, Healthy, and Delicious Cooking (available at local bookstores)
To order:
Better Homes and Gardens Reader Service
P.O. Box 9128
Dept. 9312
Des Moines, IA 50306-9128

Betty Crocker's New Choices Cookbook
Prentice Hall, New York, 1993

Pillsbury's Fast and Healthy Magazine
P.O. Box 5080
Harlan, IA 51593-0580

The Tufts University Guide to Total Nutrition
Stanley Gershoff, Ph.D.
Harper Perennial (A division of Harper Collins Publishers), 1990

Public Speaking

Fearless and Flawless Public Speaking with Power, Polish, and Pizazz
Mary-Ellen Drummond
Pfeiffer & Company, San Diego, 1993

Teamwork

ZAPP: The Lightning of Empowerment
William C. Byhan, Ph.D. with Jeff Cox
Fawcett Columbine, New York, 1988

Time and Stress Management

The Seven Habits of Highly Effective People
Stephen R. Covey
Simon & Schuster, New York, 1989

Richard Hittleman's Yoga 28 Day Exercise Plan
Richard Hittleman
Workman Publishing Company, New York, 1969

Writing and Communication

The Elements of Style
William Strunk, Jr. & E. B. White
Macmillan Publishing Co. Inc., New York, 1979

Grammar for Smart People: Your User-Friendly Guide to Speaking and Writing Better English
Barry Tarshis
Pocket Books, New York, 1992

How to Write for the World of Work
Thomas E. Pearsall & Donald Cunningham
Harcourt Brace College Publishers, Fort Worth, 1994

Punctuate It Right (2nd Ed.)
Harry Shaw
Harper Perennial, New York, 1993

Spell It Right (4th Ed.)
Harry Shaw
Harper Perennial, New York, 1993